James Armstrong

Wanny Blossoms

With a brief teatise on fishing

James Armstrong

Wanny Blossoms
With a brief teatise on fishing

ISBN/EAN: 9783337097295

Printed in Europe, USA, Canada, Australia, Japan

Cover: Foto ©Lupo / pixelio.de

More available books at **www.hansebooks.com**

"WANNY BLOSSOMS:"

A BOOK OF SONG,

WITH A BRIEF

TREATISE ON FISHING

WITH THE FLY, WORM, MINNOW, AND ROE;

Sketches of Border Life, and Fox and Otter Hunting.

BY

JAMES ARMSTRONG,

RIDSDALE, BELLINGHAM.

[COPYRIGHT.]

SECOND EDITION, ENLARGED.

Price 2s. 6d., in Extra Cloth Binding, by Post for 33 Stamps. To be had from the AUTHOR, or from the HERALD Office, Hexham.

Hexham:

PRINTED AT THE HERALD OFFICE, HALL STILE BANK.

1879.

PREFACE TO SECOND EDITION.

The welcome reception given to my first venture of "Wanny Blossoms" encourages me to give a second edition, to which I have added (in verse and prose), several new subjects, including Songs, Fishing, Fox and Otter Hunting, and other Border Sports and Pastimes, in which many of my readers doubtless take an interest.

JAMES ARMSTRONG.

Ridsdale, 30th May, 1879.

CONTENTS.

Title	Page
Wild Hills o' Wannys	1
Aid Crag	4
The Heather Bell	6
Our Glorious Borderland	8
Bonnie Banks o' Reed	10
My Muirland Hame	11
Yarrow	13
Blackburn Linn	14
Lizzie Story	15
Blithsome Mary	20
Countess of Derwentwater	21
The Flower o' Kielder	24
Renforth	25
The Scottish Lassie	27
Pencil Jack	28
Fair Joan	29
Peer Oald Joe	31
Lizzie o' the Glen	32
FISHING—	
Introductory	39
Trouting with the Fly	44
Fishing with the worm	45
Fishing with the Minnow	55
Curing of Salmon Roe, and how to fish with it	59
How to cook a trout at the river side	63
To the Fishing away	69
Dandie Dinmont and his Terriers	70
Description of Otter Hunting in the Teviot	77
Foxhunting in the Reedwater Country	83
The Bedlington Terriers	86
Otter Hunting in the Liddel and the Esk	90
Otter Hunting in the Ale	92
John Gallon	96
The celebrated Foxhounds of Emmethaugh	99
Wyndham	102
The Kielder Hunt	112
Letters to the Author	115
Gallant run with the hounds	120
The Morning Drag	124
A day with the hounds	125
The Tarsettearian Fox	129
The Trial of Wee Piper	132
Wee Piper's Letter	134
The Fishin', my Lad	136
The Wonderful Book	137
Hand away Geordy	139
Johnnie the Caller	142
The Streams o' the West	144
The Banks o' the Tyne	147
Northumbria's Pride	150
Bonnie North Tyne	154
The Charms of the Coquet	156
The Queen of the Flowers	158
Anither Sang	
Another Song	163
Anither Sang	164
Anither Sang	167
The Duel	169
Crossing the Cheviots	171

Wild Hills o' Wannys;

SINCERELY DEDICATED TO MY AFFECTIONATE BROTHER JOHN ARMSTRONG, IN COMMEMORATION OF OUR VARIED WANDERINGS TOGETHER ON THE HILLS AND BY THE STREAMS OF OUR NATIVE LAND.

The wild hills of Wannys, of which the following song is descriptive, and on whose heathery crests I first strung my rude harp, are situated between the head of the Wansbeck water and river Reed. Viewing the surrounding hills and glens from the peak of the crags, a scene of wild and majestic grandeur meets the enraptured eye, hills rising above hills on every side—Ottercaps, Hareshaw, Darna, Peaden, Simonside and Darden; on whose sides are reared Northumbria's peerless daughters and stalwart sons, and round whose base run sparkling streams, including Reed, Wansbeck, North Tyne, and Coquet, abounding with golden-spangled trout; and away to the north are the rugged crests of the Cheviots towering to the clouds and overlooking the battle fields of yore—Flodden, Chevy Chase, and Otterburn, sacred to the shades of Percy, Douglas, and Scotland's King, as also many warriors whose deeds of valour are yet recorded on the glowing scroll of fame.

Near to Wannys Crags stands Aid Crag, where the author resided for six years. It was from here, during the summer, the writer and his brothers often started with kindred spirits to run and wrestle with the shepherd lads on the heath-clad hills of Wannys, or to go a fishing excursion in the surrounding streams. And in winter, the ground all clad with snow, Sweethope Loch and adjacent rivers frozen over, we would track the otter and fox to their rocky den. It was at Dewlaw Mill, however, where I wrote the song of *Wannys*, in heartfelt devotion to the dear old spot.

O MY heart's in the west, on yon wild mossy fells,
Amang muircocks an' plovers an' red heatherbells;
Where the lambs lie in clusters on yon bonnie brae,
On the wild hills o' Wannys sae far, far away.
There's Aid Crag an' Luma, an' Hepple Heugh, too,
Hartside and Darna, I've oft been on you,
Ottercaps, Hareshaw, an' Peaden sae hie,
And the wild hills o' Wannys for ever for me.

There the muircock he becks in his wild mossy hame,
O'er the tops o' the heather ye ken his red kame;
The plover is lilting on yon mossy flowes,
The black-cock is crooing on Fernyrigg knowes.
The cranberries creep where they scarce can be seen,
The blaeberries peep frae the heather between,
An' the sweet-scented wild thyme on yon bonnie brae,
On the wild hills o' Wannys sae far, far away.

O Wannys, wild Wannys! thou rears thy proud head,
And boldly thou stands 'tween the Wansbeck and Reed,
Thou rears thy proud crest o'er hill, dale, and knowe,
Where of yore Rob o' Risinghame bent his strong bow.
The dark ravens bield on thy grey cliffs sae hie,
The fox rears her young anes, auld Wannys, in thee;
The wild flashing falcon he darts on his prey,
On the wild hills o' Wannys sae far, far away.

O Wannys, wild Wannys! the scene it is grand,
On a clear summer's morn on thy summit to stand,
The hills o'er the Carter and Cheviot to view,
An' listen the lapwing an' lonely curlew.
The shepherd he climbs thee his fair flocks to see,
An' to woo that fair mountain nymph—sweet Liberty;
On the braes by the burnie the lambs loup and play,
Round the wild hills o' Wannys sae far, far away.

Round the wild hills o' Wannys 'twas glorious to tread,
When we went otter-hunting to the Tyne or the Reed,
When *Rockwood an' Ringwood an' †Bugle's clear cry,
An' Ranger was warning the otter to die.
Then we trackt the sly fox to his den in the snow,
An' howkt him or trapt him for a grand tally ho,
And wak'd the wild echoes by Sweethope and Rae,
Round the wild hills o' Wannys sae far, far away.

Round the wild hills o' Wannys in the morn's early gleam,
O 'twas grand to gan fishing away by the Leam;
Wi' the flee o' the woodcock, the green drake, or teal,
Wi' gould speck'lt trouts we filled monie a fine creel.

  *_Rockwood, Ringwood,_ and _Ranger,_ famed otter hounds belonging to Mr. Harrison, Woodburn.
  †_Bugle,_ a celebrated otterhound, the property of William Turnbull of Bellingham.

There's the Reed an' the Wansbeck, where the dews
    sweetly fa',
The Lyles Burn and Reasey we oft fisht them a',
Aye, there's monie a burnie and sweet heather brae
Round the wild hills o' Wannys sae far, far away.

Here's to the hills o' the brave and the free,
And the red waving heather sae bonnie to see;
An' the bright gushing streams wimplin' doun to the
    dell,
By wild thyme an' gowan an' sweet heather bell;
Here's to wild Wannys' ilk hill, dale, and stream,
Still, still I am there in my thoughts an' my dream;
Here's health, peace, an' plenty, for ever and aye,
Round the wild hills o' Wannys sae far, far away.

Aid Crag.

HIGH o'er wild Wannys' lofty crest,
    Where the raven cleaves the cloud,
An' gorcocks beck around Aid Crag
    Sae crousely and sae proud,
Gurlin thro' the glens o' Reed
    Wi' a weird and eerie strum,
When round yon auld cot
    The winter winds they'd come.

When Ottercaps an' Hepple Heugh,
    Hartside and Cheviots' height,
When Peaden's peak and Darna brows
    Ance mair were clad in white,
The fox an' otter in the snaw,
    We track'd to their den,
An' when we cam to the auld cot
    We were kindly welcom'd ben,

Wi' " Fling off yer plaids an' snaw lougs,
    We've wearied for ye lang ;
Tak' a waught o' whusky, lads,
    An' sing us a guid auld sang,
Of 'Kieldar Cowt,' or 'Brandy Leash,'
    Or 'Johnnie o' Gilnockie ; '
Ye ken we like the auld sangs best,
    Sae, an auld yen let it be."

O, then we sang the auld sangs
    We'd heard the auld folks sing,
Of monie a gallant reiver clan
    Wha fear'd nae Lord nor King ;
But harried the faulds baith far an' wide
    Of wether, cowt, an' steer ;
An' when at need could wield the brand,
    An' poise the Border spear.

An' aye we sang o' the auld times,
    An' monie a tale we tauld
Of Tyne, and Reed, and Liddesdale,
    An' moss-troopers sae bauld ;

Of midnight raid, an' morning fight,
  By grey peel, cairn, or stream,
Till fancy heard the slogan wild,
  And saw the bright steel gleam.

An' aye we tauld the fairy tales,
  And sang the rebel sangs
Of dauntless Derwentwater's doom,
  An' the exil'd Stuart's wrangs;
We tauld of "Barty o' the Kame,"
  "Red Cap,' and Bowrie too,
An' sang of "Rob o' Risinghame,"
  Until the grey cock crew.

The Heather Bell.

DEDICATED TO LEWIS PROUDLOCK, THE BORDER MINSTREL.

Thou bonnie, bonnie heather bell,
  That blooms sae fair an' free!
Thou glads my soul, thou lovely gem,
  Where'er thy bells I see.
Sae sweet thou blows on Kielder braes,
  An' round the Pecrie Well,
On Wannys' brows an' Sweethope flowes,
  My bonnie heather bell.

The mountain bee sucks life frae thee,
    Around the lonesome dells ;
The western breezes sweetly sigh,
    An' kiss thy bonnie bells ;
The lavrock sings a song o' love,
    High, high o'er stream an' stell ;
The braes a' sound wi' joy around
    My bonnie heather bell.

In ither lands I've wander'd far,
    Ayont the Atlantic tide,
An' seen bright flowers o' gaudy hue,
    By the dark Beaver's side ;
In trackless woods an' prairies wide,
    Far frae my native dell,
It made me wae I couldna see
    My bonnie heather bell.

The lavrock's song it wasna there,
    Nor robin's, on the thorn ;
Nae muircock's beck nor blackcock's croo,
    Or sound of mountain horn.
An' O ! my fancy saw thee still,
    Fair flower, on mossy fell ;
Light is my heart, nae mair we'll part,
    My bonnie heather bell !

Our Glorious Borderland.

**DEDICATED (BY PERMISSION) TO OUR BORDER CHIEF,
W. H. CHARLTON, OF HESLEYSIDE.**

On Monkside's wild and lofty heights,
    Where roves the mountain bee,
Here blooms the bonnie heather bell,
    An' muircocks whirring flee.
An' O! what sounds o' liberty
    I hear, on every hand,
An' view ance mair the hills an' dales
    Of our Glorious Borderland.

I've seen the spangl'd banner wave
    Ayont Lake Ontario's tide;
An' chas'd the deer an' panther wild,
    By the deep Beaver's* side:
But aye my fancy wander'd back,
    When on a foreign strand,
To the Dandie Dinmonts on the hills
    Of our Glorious Borderland.

It glads my heart ance mair to see
    The glens o' Reed and Tyne,
Of Wansbeck, Coquet, Tarset, too,
    The Liddell and the Lyne;

    * *Beaver*, a river in North America.

Where rugged tower an' moss-gray keep,
   And castles proudly stand,
Where monie heroes mouldering sleep,
   In our Glorious Borderland.

Nae mair adown yon lonely dells
   Will dauntless Bowrie ride,
Or " Kinmont Willie," " Gilnockie,"
   Nor brave " Jock o' the Syde,"
By Border Peel, in glittering steel,
   Wi' a true and gallant band;—
My heart yet swells o' them to tell,
   In our Glorious Borderland.

The "Wily Brows," the " Harper Flowes,"
   And " Archer Cleuch," I see,
Where " Cowt o' Kieldar " rang'd of yore,
   Ower a' yon wilds sae free,
Wi' his true brother " Brandy Leash,"
   Wi' arrow, bow, and brand,
Oft fang'd the red-deer and the wolf,
   In our Glorious Borderland.

An' yonder's Darden's dusky peak,
   And Wanny's sunny brow,
Beside were sparkling crystal streams
   An' mountain burnies flow;
An' Cheviot's wild and shaggy crest,
   High o'er them a' sae grand,
O'er " Chevy Chase " and " Otterburn,"
   In our Glorious Borderland.

Of Flodden Field we yet will sing,
　　And of dread Waterloo:
Where Border lions strew'd the sward
　　Wi' monie a gallant foe;
Their heather crests ran in their breasts,
　　As they stript the flashing brand;
And their crimson'd laurels proudly bore,
　　To our Glorious Borderland.

Bonnie Banks o' Reed.

Air: "The Harp that once through Tara's Halls."

The snaw's a' gane frae Peaden-hill,
　　Sweet Spring returns ance mair,
An' strews the wild flowers o'er the dale,
　　Sae lovely and sae fair.
The primrose by fair Lyles-burn side
　　'Peeps oot wi' modest head;
And the daisy decks the green sward
　　On the bonnie banks o' Reed.

O but the scene is fair and grand,
　　To stray down by the Leam,
When morn first breaks o'er Ottercaps,
　　And lights on hill a:' stream;

When the throssle whistles on the bough,
   An' the lark his pinions spread,
Up heavenward, wi' joyfu' sang,
   Frae the bonnie banks o' Reed.

O for ane hour on Hepple Heugh,
   Where often I hae been,
Reclining on yon mossy knowe,
   To view the lovely scene;
The bounding pulse of liberty
   Wad then ance mair be freed,
While pondering on youth's early prime,
   On the bonnie banks o' Reed.

My Muirland Hame.

**INSCRIBED TO MY CLANSMAN, THOMAS ARMSTRONG
OF THE LOW LEAZES.**

*(Written when the Author was on the banks of the
Beaver River, North America.)*

My bonnie, bonnie Muirland hame,
   I rue that I left thee,
An' a' Northumbria's hills and dales,
   To cross the Atlantic sea.
O! gie me back my knowes an' flowes,
   And tak yer wealth and fame,
Yer boundless woods, and prairies wide, —
   Gie me my muirland hame.

My heart is yet in Borderland,
   By streams an' sunny braes,
Where wildly wave the heatherbells
   In the bright morning rays;
Where a' my dauntless clansmen true,
   That bear Gilnockie's name,
Still proudly tell o' days of yore,
   Around my muirland hame.

Could I but see my Wannys wild,
   An' hear the lavrocks sing;
Could I but see yon heathery dell
   Where the blae-berries hing;
The muircock's beck could I but hear,
   And see his bonnie kame,
Or hear the heather-bleater hie
   Around my muirland hame.

Nae sparkling streams, nae yellow trouts,
   Nae heather-bells are here;
Nor lammies loupin on the braes,
   My longing soul to cheer.
O bear me back! thou gallant ship,
   Across the briny faem;
That I may see my mountains free,
   My bonnie muirland hame.

Yarrow.

Awake, awake my silent harp,
    Awaken frae thy slumbers,
And we will sing of Yarrow braes
    In wild an' gladsome numbers.
Sweet Liberty, that banner fair
    Unfurl, my "winsome marrow,"
The wind shall wave thy gowden hair
    O'er the bonny braes of Yarrow.

Although the sleet and misty weet
    On Yarrow fell are falling,
The auld muircocks on heath'ry knowes
    Round Yarrow yet are calling;
The robin on the stuntit thorn
    Trills sweetly on the morrow,
The hunter winds his blithesome horn
    By the bonnie braes of Yarrow.

The fox is up, the hounds full cry,
    Their glorious notes are swelling,
The echo's wild thro' shaggy glens
    An' o'er the dusky Belling.

And see yon gallant Border band
    Thro' wide streams and the narrow,
The Sistersons amang the van,
    The Sistersons of Yarrow.

An' O! 'tis sweet on Yarrow braes,
    When flowrets wild are springing,
To fish fair Tyne for yellow trout,
    And hear the throssles singing.
An' O! to see the wimplin burns,
    That rin yon glens a' thorough,
When nature brings the lavrock's wings
    O'er the bonnie braes of Yarrow.

Blackburn Linn.

O SWEETLY flows the lovely Reed,
Where heather grows and gorcocks feed;
Her sparkling waters rippling rin
By the budding birks of Blackburn Linn.

Thou bonnie Linn, when summer comes
Thy brows are clad wi' heather-blooms;
Sae softly sighs the western win'
To kiss thy flow'rets, Blackburn Linn.

Fair flow'rets o' the rainbow's hue,
The wild rose, gowan, an' violet blue,
Bloom by thy water's gladsome din,
Thou bonnie, bonnie Blackburn Linn.

The lavrock spreads his dewy wings,
An o'er thy dusky bosom sings,
The spangled trout wi' quivering fin
Sport in thy streamlet, Blackburn Linn.

The otter kens a hame in thou,
The wily fox and foumart too,
Thy rugged rocks they shelter in,
Thou bonnie, bonnie Blackburn Linn.

Lizzie Storey.

The subject of the following song was a servant girl at Parkside, near Bardon Mill, Northumberland. The only other occupant of the house being an old lady, for whom Lizzie acted in the double capacity of servant and companion. During the month of October, 1867, Bardon Mill and vicinity was visited by two notorious burglars, named Finney and Adamson, for whom the police were diligently searching after for previous crimes.

Parkside, from its lonely and isolated situation, attracted the notice of the two villians, who, after reconnoitring, and being satisfied as to an easy accomplishment of their evil designs, set their plans in motion for the ransacking of the lonely homestead, between the hours of twelve and one, on the morning of the 24th October.

The house was entered by Adamson, admittance being gained by extracting the dairy window; Finney keeping watch without in order to prevent surprise, as likewise to hinder the escape of the inmates to raise an alarm.

The noise of their operations awakened the ever alert and watchful Lizzie. Springing from bed, she seized a broomstick, and began a search of the house, followed by her enfeebled mistress. On coming to the dairy, they were confronted by Adamson. It was at this juncture that Lizzie showed one of the most striking examples of undaunted courage and noble daring that we have on record. Not thinking for one moment of her dishabille, she struck out right and left with the stick; and so effective was the onslaught, that the cowardly ruffian, finding himself worsted in the fight, seized a scythe, and with it aimed a deadly blow at the heroic girl; warding it off, at the same time receiving a severe cut across the hand, she closed with her burly antagonist, who, finding the ungainly weapon of no advantage in close quarters, cast it aside, and seizing the girl by the hair, dragged and kicked her in a most unmerciful and brutal manner along the floor. In this desperate situation the undaunted girl's bravery and presence of mind still showed forth, as she called to her terror-stricken mistress: "Get the scissors and cut my hair!" to free her from the hands of the assailant. Before this could be done, she extricated herself, and tearing the mask from off the burglar's face, remarked that she would know him again. By this time Finney was endeavouring to enter by the kitchen window. Seeing this, our heroine got hold of an old gun, and pointed it at the robber's breast, but being an old-fashioned flint lock, it missed fire; throwing it quickly aside she seized the poker, and used it with such success that the two villians beat a hasty retreat.

Information being given to the police, they immediately set off in pursuit, and subsequently captured Adamson at Annfield Plain; while Finney, actuated by some strange infatuation or motive of revenge, like a blood-thirsty tiger, still lurked about Parkside, where he was met by Sergt. Young, of the Northumberland Constabulary, who at once charged him with the crime, and proceeded to take him into custody. This was no easy task; and after a desperate struggle, in which the officer received very serious injury, Finney managed to escape. His liberty, however, was of short duration, for on the following morning he was captured at Whitshields, and conveyed to Hexham lock-up, 9th Dec., 1867. Here he succeeded in breaking out, but was soon recaptured, tried, and sentenced with Adamson to fifteen years penal servitude.

At the trial of the prisoners, when Lizzie had concluded her evidence, his Lordship said: "You deserve great commendation for your courage and fidelity to your mistress." And at the rising of the court he said to Lizzie that "her conduct deserved something more than mere verbal praise. He had found that the law allowed him to do something more. She would be paid £5 as a reward for her fidelity and courage to her mistress. She had behaved so gallantly on the occasion, that it reminded him of some story of romance, rather than an incident of every-day life."

The inhabitants of the neighbourhood, desiring a more solid memorial of the girl's exemplary bravery and heroic courage, presented her with a silver tea-service, accompanied with a handsome silver vase, bearing the following inscription:—"Presented to Elizabeth Storey, as a token of esteem for her heroic conduct with the burglars at Parkside, on the night of the 24th October, 1867."

STRIKE the wild harp, ye bards of fame, and sing
    along with me,
In measure bold the truth unfold o'er mountain,
    dale, and lea;
My song is not of Highland chief, or knight of
    Palestine,

But of a female brave and bold—a dauntless heroine.

CHORUS:

Gallant Lizzie Storey, we'll drink her health in wine,
Northumbria's pride and glory—that dauntless heroine.

Like wolves that range the desert far in dark and dreary night,
To plunder Parkside's lonely bield two robbers do unite,
Where no one save an aged dame and this brave girl do dwell;
And to sing of her gallant deed my heart with pride doth swell.

In at the dairy window now one robber doth appear,
Of woman's arm he dreads no harm, he enters without fear;
Like lioness that guards her young deep in the jungle lands,
So dauntless now our heroine before the robber stands.

Now blow for blow she gives the foe, so dauntless and alone,
No martial voice nor beat of drum is there to cheer her on;

Wild is the game, the blood doth flow, still
    gallantly stands she;
Wild is the strife of death or life, of life and victory.

The robber now, with coward hand, doth seize her
    flowing hair,
And throws her down, and drags her round, and
    strikes her here and there;
She's up! see, see her rise again, and like Britannia
    stand—
She tears the mask from off his face so gallant
    and so grand.

To help his comrade in the strife, the outside
    robber now,
With crash an' slash and deadly oath, the window's
    coming through;
Still with a weapon in her hand, she strikes him
    gallantly;
He and his coward comrade now, they for their
    lives do fly.

Weave, weave a wreath of laurel, Northumbria's
    daughters fair,
Entwine it with the tartan and heather-bell so
    rare;
Place it on Lizzie Storey's brow, that fought so
    gallantly,
And crown our dauntless heroine the Queen of
    Victory.

Blithesome Mary.

BLITHESOME Mary o' the Glen
Singin' but an' laughin' ben ;
Heart as true as Border steel,
Lythe o' limb an' light o' heel,
Brow as bright as morning skies,
Ruby lips and hazel eyes.
O to see the cantie queen,
In the bonnie tartan sheen,
Trippin' like a Monkside fairy
O'er the bent sae blithe an' airy;
Liltin o'er the auld Scots ballants,
Daffin wi' the hunter callants.
Weel can the sonsie lassie tell
O' a' the hunts on Kielder fell ;—
Loupin' on the bare-back'd steed,
Dashin' past wi' falcon speed !
O to see the ploy sae rare,
Beamin' e'e an' flowing hair;
Singin' but an' dancin' ben,
Winsome Mary o' the glen.

Countess of Derwentwater.

Dedicated (by permission) to Amelia, Countess of Derwentwater, Baroness of Langley and Tynedale.

AIR: "The Tartan Plaid."

A NOBLE dame, her rights to claim,
   Is come, a Radcliffe's dauntless daughter;
Of glorious name and spotless fame,—
   Amelia, Countess of Derwentwater.

CHORUS;

Over the brave may the proud flag wave,
Over the Countess proudly wave.

In Dilston's fair and lordly halls,
   Earl Derwentwater dwelt in splendour;
And his Lady bright, with her dauntless Knight
   And gallant hearts for to defend her.

Till the cry of war came from afar,
   By the exil'd Stuart proclaim'd fairly;
To claim his own—the British Crown—
   The Royal Prince they lov'd so dearly.

Then war-steeds pranc'd, and banners danc'd,
   And warlike men came late and early,
With white cockades, and glittering blades,
   To fight for the Prince they lov'd so dearly.

When the Lady fair, with playful smile,
   Held forth her hand, so white and pearly—
"My gallant Lord, give me your sword,
   And I'll fight for the Prince we love so dearly."

His lion valour thus arous'd,
   Unto his lady said right fairly—
"A Radcliffe's name and a Radcliffe's fame,
   Shall live with the Prince we love so dearly."

The Earl of Mar, like the god of war,
   With his kilted clansmen marching rarely,
To the sound of drum and the pibroch's strum,
   Went to fight for the Prince they lov'd so dearly.

At Preston town, for his Prince and crown,
   So dauntlessly fought Derwentwater;
But by false friends and treachery,
   The brave and true had to surrender.*

---

* The news of the intended surrender filled the great body of the common soldiers with the deepest indignation. The Highlanders especially were terribly enraged, and declared they would die sword in hand, and insisted on making an attempt to cut their way through the Royal forces. Had Mr Forster (the leader of the Northern army) appeared in the streets, he would have been slain, though he had had an hundred lives. As it

For treason tried, condemn'd to die,
   Which grieved the nation's heart full sorely;
In his youth and bloom, sad was his doom,
   For the brave Prince he lov'd so dearly.

No more fair Dilston towers he saw,
   Nor Tyne's fair stream, that runs so clearly;
Nor his Lady† bright, his heart's delight,—
   He died for the Prince he lov'd so dearly.

was, he narrowly escaped being killed in his own room. A Scottish gentleman, named Murray, who had waited upon him to remonstrate against the surrender, was so enraged as to fire a pistol at him; and but for the prompt interposition of Mr Patten, who struck up Murray's arm at the moment of the discharge, the ball would certainly have pierced Forster's body.

† If the Countess of Derwentwater had by her influence brought the Earl into his present dangerous state she now exerted herself heroically to save him. On Sunday, the 10th of February, accompanied by the Duchesses of Cleveland, Bolton, and Buccleuch, and other ladies of the highest rank, she went to St. James's palace, and as the King was returning from the chapel, knelt before him and implored mercy for his noble captive. Her prayer for the royal intercession was supported by the ladies who accompanied her; but George I. was not of a nature to be moved by such piteous appeals. It is tolerably certain that the prayer of the Earl's gentle advocates was heard with aversion by King George. The Earl's consanguinity to the exiled House of Stuart was of itself an offence which the occupier of the Stuart's throne could not forgive; besides, the historic page on which his dark and portentous shadow is cast records that he was incapable of generosity towards any but favourites and mistresses; that he was arrogant and imperious as he was ignorant, immoral, and depraved. The Peers, who on the following Wednesday ventured to advocate mercy to the Earl, incurred King George's marked displeasure.

On Tower Hill they his blood did spill,
   On Tower Hill they him did slaughter;
For his land and gold, his life was sold,
   The brave young Earl of Derwentwater.

The Flower o' Kielder.

White Kielder flows where milk-white yowes
   Are feeding on yon benty hill;
An' the shepherd, wi' his bleating lambs,
   Is lying by the mountain rill.
His leal young heart is wi' the lass
   That wanders by the Sheil o' Brann;
Love in her e'e, an' footsteps free,
   She's the Flower o' Kielder, bonnie Ann.

Where the heather bell round cairn an' stell,
   Where daisies peep frae sunny braes,
Where red noops grow an' moss-roses blow,—
   It's there the comely lassie strays,
Like Nature's sel', to view her treasures,
   Or Flora in a fairy lan',
Wi' her gowden hair in tresses fair,
   She's the Flower o' Kielder, bonnie Ann.

Where gowans sweet in the dewy weet,
    Where cowslips and primroses bloom,
Where the dew-drop hings on the blue-bell's rim,
    An' the wild thyme springs, she loves to roam.
When the lavrock spreads his wings in rapture,
    An' sings his sang to heaven's span,—
His joyfu' sang o' liberty,
    To the Flower o' Kielder, bonnie Ann.

Where e'er the lovely lassie wander,
    Wi' Eden fair it seems to vie;
An' O! the scene o' glorious grandeur,
    Might bring an angel frae the sky.
Sing thy sweet sang, thou lark, in gladness,
    Bloom flow'rets fair on ilka han',
Flow sparkling streams in sunny beams,
    For the Flower o' Kielder, bonnie Ann.

Renforth.

SEE yonder gallant band,
Leaving the English strand,
And away to a strange land,
    To ply the fleet oar;
With Renforth their captain brave,
Over the bounding wave,
Proud Albion's fame to save,
    On Columbia's wild shore,

Mark then yon eager crowd,
List to that hurrah loud,
See now the rivals proud,
    For the contest prepare,
See from Lake Huron's tide,
From forest and prairie wide,
Cheering by the white man's side,
    The red-skin is there.

See, see the British crew
Stretch to their oars so true,
Over the waters blue,
    With falcon-wing speed,
O! what stays their leader's hand?
O! what foils his stroke once grand?
Is it Fate's dread command,
    Or Treachery's foul deed?

Weep, child and widow young;
Tell, Bard, in mournful song,
How in his pride so strong,
    So nobly fell he;
Pulling against grim death,
On to his latest breath,—
Clouded is the victor's wreath,
    With dark mystery.

The Scottish Lassie.

[This song was one of the Author's earliest productions.]

ANEATH the dusky peak o' Cheviot,
   Where the falcon spreads his flashing wings,
Where the wild thyme springs, and blue-bells
    blossom,
   And the lavrock o'er the yowe-bught sings;
Where the fox-foot creeps, and the blackcock
    croos,
   By auld gray stell and mossy stane,—
There I o'erhied the Scottish Lassie,
   Gaun a yowe-milking a' alane.

Her sonsie brow sae brent an' bonnie;
   Her skin was like the lilies fair;
Her eyes were like the sparkling diamonds;
   Her lips were like the rubies rare;
Round her wee mou' were lovely dimples;
   Her cheeks were o' the moss-rose hue;
While o'er her snow-white neck in freedom,
   Her yellow hair in ringlets flew.

The Scottish Lass was clad sae sweetly,
  In tartans o' the blue and green;
As bare-fit o'er the bent she trippit,—
  I trow she was a comely queen.
Sweet innocence in every feature;
  Fair emblem o' true liberty;—
I'll ne'er forget the Scottish Lassie,
  And the Cheviots wild, till the day I dee.

Pencil Jack.

Jack has been a sodger brave,
  An' he's been in the wars;
Noo he's return'd, wi' glory crown'd,
  And monie wounds and scars.
His cuts are a' afore his face,
  An' nane ahint his back,
An' that in the right place, my lad;
  He's a hero, Pencil Jack.

Jack is turn'd a merchant noo,
  He deals in needles an' pins,
Envelopes, paper, and pencils, too,
  Laces, braces, and skins.

He nacks his heels, an' round he wheels,
    An' gies his thooms a crack ;
Sae neat and slick he twirls the stick,—
    Hurrah for Pencil Jack !

Jack's as happy as a king,
    An' Pencil Mag a queen ;
They range the Borders up and down,
    Baith far and near they've been ;
By Kielderhead and down the Reed,
    They bauldly tak the track ;
Sic sprees an' ploys an' rambling joys,
    Hae Mag an' Pencil Jack.

Fair Joan.

BESIDE yon high and heathery mountain,
    Where the burnie wimples by the brae,
An' the sun's mild rays by fell and fountain
    A' Nature wakes at early day.
Fair Flora there her flow'rets strewing,
    Down the dewy dells on ilka han',
An' the cuckoo's note is saftly wooing
    The Border blossom, fair Joan.

Her eyes are like the beam o' morning
    When the mavis whistles on the spray;
Mild innocence her face adorning,
    The young and winsome Queen o' May.
Auld Monkside's crest is towering proudly
    O'er the fairest flower in a' wer lan',
As if to guard the lovely lassie,
    The Border blossom, fair Joan.

O weel befa' the comely creature,
    Her father's care, an' her mither's pride;
Her brither's pet, and yon yauld lad's darling
    That tents his flocks on the mountain side.
'Mid scenes o' wild an' rugged grandeur,
    As if toucht by some fairy wan',
To the lovely lass his thoughts oft wander,
    The Border blossom, fair Joan.

Pour thy wae note thou lanesome pliver,
    Toot thy sweet horn thou mountain bee;
Ye shy curlew and heather-bleater,
    Join in the glorious melody.
Trill thy sweet lay thou wee mosscheeper,
    Ye lavrocks sing in the carol gran',
Swell the heavenly chorus roun' an' roun'
    The Border blossom fair Joan.

Peer Oald Joe.

(In the Cumberland Dialect.)

Up in the moornein at hoaf-past five,
Killin' his sel' ta keep himsel' alive;
Bent hoaf dubbil, en' snow-wheyte heed;
Peer oald fella, he'd better be deed.
Haggin' in watter, en' kairyin kwoals,
Tummelin' inta th' gutters en' hwoals.
Stouterin' thro' beath sleet en' snow,—
As hard as an otter is peer oald Joe.

Inta the shop at hoaf-past six,
Blooin' the bellas en' sharpin' th' picks;
He mun hev them oa deun at hoaf-past eight,
Or else the back-men 'ill skowld en' feight.
Then ta th' hoos he mun slip elang,
For a lal sup tea ta mak him strang;
But in his heaste he's gitten a foa,
En' brocken his shins, hes peer oald Joe.

Limpin' elang ta th' hoos et last—
But theer's neabody in, en' th' dour it's fast;
He knocks wud his foot, en' he jingles the sneck,
If he beyds ower lang he'll git the seck.

He wags his heed en' cocks oot his chin,
En' says what he'll dee if he nobbit gets in—
He'll pack up his duds en' leave them oa,
En' ga tull Amerryka, peer oald Joe.

Back ta th' shop, en' inta th' neuk,
En' oot wud th' peype for a lal bit smeak.
They cry, "What fettle, Joe? are ye well?"
"Oh, furst-rate, neycely; Hoo's yersel'?"
It's Freyday noo, en' th' pay's th' neet,
When a lal sup yall 'ill put Joe oa reet;
Whe then 'ill be peartest emang them oa,
Whe laffin' en' jwoakin'—but peer oald Joe!

Lizzie o' the Glen.

BLITHE, blithe is the beam o' her bonnie blue e'e,
An' o'er her fair shoothers her linty locks flee;
Wi' light fairy footsteps wha laughin' comes ben?
It's lovely young Lizzie o' yon bonnie glen.

Wi' her lips like the cherries, sae red-ripe, I trow,
Or the scarlet noop-berries that on Cheviot grow;
Like the sweet blushing rose-bud in yon dewy fen,
Is lovely young Lizzie o' yon bonnie glen.

O the fair sonsie queen, wi' her bright sunny brow,
An' twa bonnie dimples near her comely mou',
She's the flower o' the muirlands, that's tauld by
    ilk ane,
When they sing o' young Lizzie o' yon bonnie glen.

Yon yauld hunter lad kythes the first break o' morn,
On the wild peaks o' Monkside he winds his clear
    horn;
What ails the leal callant? troth, he disna ken,
When he sighs for young Lizzie o' yon bonnie glen.

Thou gray speckl'd lark, shake the weet frae thy
    wing,
Rise high to the blue lift and sweet, sweetly sing;
Awaken ye sangsters in ilk bushy den,
And sing to young Lizzie o' yon bonnie glen.

FISHING.

INTRODUCTORY.

THERE is no sport on which more diversity of opinion exists than Angling. Fishing of any kind, may be summed up in knowing what to fish with; when, how, and where to fish.

Having fished the most of our Border streams: including, the Reed, Tyne, Wansbeck, Coquet, Kielder, Jed, Liddel, Tweed, Teviot, Till, and Whiteadder, as also other streams; and in my wanderings have met some of the most intelligent and successful anglers of the Borders, among whom I may mention, Mr Robert Allen, the Armstrongs of Bellingham; Mr Morrison, Kelso; Mr Thomas Brydon, Plashetts; Mr Mavin, of Rothbury; Mr J. Thompson, of Hexham; Mr R, Thompson, of Otterburn; Mr Clark, of Harbottle: Mr Gibson, the traveller, and may include one from whom I received many useful lessons in the "Gentle Art," namely, my brother, Sergeant J. Armstrong, of Ford.

Often have I had the pleasure of witnessing these gentlemen's brilliant illustrations of angling, and listened with intense delight to the exposition of their varied ideas regarding the habits of the fish, as also the attractive virtue of this and that lure; which, combined with practical experience, and the written authority of other true and devoted piscatorial disciples of the world-renowned Isaac Walton, has warranted me in venturing to give a few brief and useful instructions upon the subject, in a condensed form. I have not attempted to give the various perplexing methods of capturing fish, supposed to constitute the finished angler. They are simply a combination of practice and oral information, interspersed with select extracts from Stewart's Practical Angler and Stoddart's Angler's Companion, which authorities are at the service and within the reach of every one having leisure and inclination to seek out and arrange, a task more difficult than I at first anticipated, but when complete, form a summary of correct and useful information, which, I surmise, will attract and interest such of my readers as are lovers of the delightful sport of Trout Fishing.

ON TROUTING WITH THE FLY.

The first subject which naturally suggests itself is the rod and tackle most suitable for fly-fishing. The two great requisites in a rod are stiffness and lightness, qualities exceedingly difficult to combine. Great difference of opinion exists as to how a rod should be put together; but the tie system is by far the best. A tied rod is not so apt to break as one with brass joints, and also bends more equally throughout, and is therefore the most agreeable one to use. A rod of eleven feet is about the best length for fly-fishing; and when put up should yield slightly from a little above the hand to the top, and balance about a foot from above the hand.

With regard to the wheel line, good chestnut coloured hair is best. After the wheel line, there should be a casting line composed of six lengths of triple gut, twisted together. This can only be properly made by a machine for the purpose. Only the longest threads should be used, and as nearly as possible of one thickness. Before attaching them to the machine, they should be soaked in cold water for half an hour, or they will break in the process of twisting. The most secure method of joining them is with the single slip knot, and lapping the ends over with well waxed thread, a little spirit varnish makes all secure. The fly-cast should be joined to the casting line, by four lengths of picked gut, tapering in thickness to where the fly-tackle is attached.

In making up a fly cast, lay the ends of the threads of gut side by side, and simply knot the one round the other; in the right direction it will hold together, but may be separated by pulling the short ends. The above is the single slip knot. The double slip knot is so far the same, but in knotting the threads round each other, the ends are passed twice through instead of once; this, if properly done, makes by far the neatest joining, and can be drawn asunder, a dropper taken off and another substituted in its place. A single knot, not more than two inches from the hook, inserted between the closing ends, will hold the dropper quite secure. The distance between the flies should be twenty-two inches.

And here, I wish to call the attention of the angler to the most important subject connected with his tackle; and that is the gut. For angling in clear water, inhabited by cunning cautious trout, *fine thin gut* is absolutely necessary for success.

All gut is, more or less, of a clear colour, which glitters in the sun; and in order to divest it of this, it requires to be stained. To attain this, boil a handful of logwood in a pint of water, and add copperas till it is of a bluish green tint, a piece of copperas about the size of a pea will be sufficient. If too much is put in it will make it quite blue. The gut should be put into the liquid when cold, and allowed to remain till of the required colour.

As regards flies for trouting purposes; this is a subject involving such a variety of ideas in different anglers that, to describe the features, which characterize and distinguish each kind of fly, is utterly impossible. Simply for this reason, they baffle all power of description, and any attempt to do so would only perplex the reader. Therefore, I shall at once go straight to the mark, and give what I have found to be a killing fly-stock—

        1.—The Woodcock.
        2.—The Teal.
        3.—The Green Drake.
        4.—The Dotterel.
        5.—The Red-hackle, or Red Spider.
        6.—The Black-hackle, or Black Spider.

Experience has taught me to consider the above diversities of flies as unsurpassed. It may be very true, however, as I have already said, that many anglers give preference to more perplexing varieties. And when in possession of such, it is here where the fly-fisher often makes the mistake, when the trout are on the feed, by consuming the primest portions of the day in testing the attractive power of this and that fly; now taking off one because he thinks it a shade too dark; now another, because he thinks it too large; and attaching, in turn, as many different kinds of fly as would stock a fishing-tackle shop. And to upset such erroneous notions, I may safely affirm that one or other of the flies above specified may be employed with a fair measure of success on Coquet, Reed, Tyne, Wansbeck, or any of our Border streams.

In April, the angler must look for sport in the pools, as the trout are not yet strong enough to lie in the streams, therefore, it is no use fishing in them. There are some parts of a pool in which trout are more likely to be found than others. There are always plenty of them lying in the shallow water at the pool foot; which, if there is a ripple on it, will be found to be the best place of all. In cold weather, in the early part of the season, the sunny side of the water is where feeding trout are to be found.

Passing from April to May, trout improve greatly

in condition, and move into the stronger water, about the heads of pools, and scatter themselves through the streams. At this season of the year, it is of little use attempting fly-fishing before nine in the morning; from nine till two is the best time, after that they generally leave off taking; but commence again in the evening if the weather is mild. Towards the end of the month, a showery day is best, with a south or west wind.

The best condition of water for capturing trout is when of an amber colour. If it is only coloured or slightly swollen, trout will be found in the same places as when it is clear; but, when the water is large and dark coloured, it is of no use fishing the streams, as they are too rapid; and in the pools the trout are all congregated about the sides. In such circumstances, therefore, the angler should not waste time fishing the centre of the pool, but merely fish the sides; fishing the side he is on straight up, and as near to the side as possible, and the opposite side partly up and partly across.

The flies used in May should be smaller than those used in April. If the waters are clear, No. 11 or 12 size of hook will answer very well; but if the water is coloured, a size larger may be used, as a good sized fly will catch the best trout in heavy water. Towards the end of May the trout are in prime condition, strong and vigorous. They now forsake the deeper portions of the pools, moving up into the strong water at the head, and into broken water and streams; where they choose convenient feeding stations, such as eddies, behind stones, below banks, and tufts of grass; in short, every place where they can remain unseen and watch for their prey, as it comes down stream towards them; and the angler should neglect no place where he thinks it likely for a feeding trout to be.

Streams should be fished in exactly the same manner as pools; fishing the side you are on straight up, and the opposite side partly up and partly across. All quiet water between two streams, and eddies behind stones, should also be carefully fished. It is more difficult fishing streams than pools, as it requires more nicety in casting. Casting partly across and partly up stream, for a variety of reasons, is more deadly than casting directly up. The advantages of having a number of flies is entirely lost by casting straight up, as they all come down in one line, and it is only the trout in that line that see them; whereas, if thrown partly across, they all come down in different lines, and the trout in all these lines see them. A trout on seizing an artificial fly, is instantaneously aware that it is counterfeit, and never attempts to swallow it, frequently letting it go before the angler has time to strike; so it is of the utmost importance to strike immediately, and this is the reason why a quick eye and a ready hand are considered the most necessary qualifications for a fly-fisher.

A trout takes a fly and makes the motion termed a rise, which consists of their turning to go down; the angler therefore does not see the break on the surface until the trout has either seized or missed the fly; so that he has already lost so much time, and should strike immediately.

Striking should be done by a slight but quick motion of the wrist, not by any motion of the arm, and to strike in the direction the rod is moving at the time. In fishing up, the rise of a trout is by no means so distinct as in fishing down. They frequently seize the fly without breaking the surface, and the first intimation the angler gets of their presence is a pull at the line. The utmost attention is therefore necessary, to strike the *moment* the least motion is either seen or felt. This is in some measure owing to the flies being in general a little under water, but principally to the fact that trout take a fly coming down stream in a quieter and more deadly manner than a fly going up. Seeing it going up stream, they seem afraid it may escape, make a rush, and in their hurry to seize very frequently miss it altogether. It is very different fishing up stream; the trout see the fly coming towards them, rise to meet it and seize it, without any dash, but in a firm deadly manner. Another advantage of this mode of fishing is that it does not disturb the water so much. Let us suppose the angler is fishing down a fine pool. He of course commences at the top, the place where the best trout and those inclined to feed invariably lie. After a few casts he hooks one, which immediately runs down – and by its leaping in the air and plunging in all directions alarms all its neighbours, and it is ten to one he gets another rise in that pool. Fishing up saves all this. The fisher begins at the foot, and when he hooks a trout pulls it down, and the remaining portions of the pool are undisturbed.

From about the latter end of May to the beginning of August is the worst part of the whole season for fly-fishing in large rivers; in the hill streams however it is different, as there the trout never seem to tire of anything in the shape of surface food, as I have been informed by Mr. William Douglas, gamekeeper to his Grace the Duke of Northumberland, that he has frequently seen the trout eagerly rising at and seizing the feathers that fell from the hawks which he shot about the Linns of Skaap Burn and White Kielder Water.

As I have already stated, the months of June and July afford but indifferent sport to the fly-fisher frequenting our larger streams. During these months, however, he will find a killing lure in the worm.

ON FISHING WITH THE WORM FOR TROUT.

Of the various lures for trout, the worm unquestionably ranks among the foremost. The season for worm-fishing seldom commences until the latter end of May, or beginning of June, when the main streams and their tributaries are, in ordinary seasons, considerably reduced. June and July, added to the latter end of May, constitute our best worm-fishing months.

I am not alluding to the simple and coarse practice of the art, as pursued in flooded and discoloured streams, among hungry unwary fish. I treat of it solely as respects clear waters inhabited by cunning cautious trout, and in consequence, as a method of angling, requires of the craftsman great skill, consummate address, and no stinted amount of practice, prudence, and patience.

The angler who can capture trout when the waters are low and clear, the skies bright, and atmosphere warm, will have no difficulty in filling his creel in a flooded stream. I heartily concur with Stoddart and Stewart, those accomplished anglers and brilliant writers on the subject, when they assert that fishing in clear water is the only branch of the art that ought to be dignified by the name of sport.

Angling and butchering fish I consider two totally different occupations. For my own part, I would rather capture eight or nine pounds of well fed, plump trout, than twenty pounds of lank, lean, big-headed fish, such as are to be met with in the Tarset.

And as a contrast to the above-named rivulet, I may mention the far famed Coquet, which is unquestionably one of the finest trouting streams on the Borders; and of all the streams that I am acquainted with, is, moreover, the most amply stocked with trout. The Coquet trout externally is a beautiful fish: the back is finely curved, the head small and of a fine golden-olive tint, the stars on each side being of a purple hue. And I may observe that there is a marked resemblance existing between the trout of the Coquet, Liddel, and Whiteadder.

As regards the sister streams—Reed and North Tyne, the trout frequently to be met with in them unite the characteristics belonging to the fish of each river, and are deeply shaped, small headed trout. The outward complexion of the sides is yellow, beautifully bespangled with stars or beads of a deep crimson colour. And with regard to the neighbouring stream, the Wansbeck, the same observation holds good.

Regarding clear water fishing, the first subject is the rod and tackle most suitable for the purpose; this merits very strict attention. The rod should not be shorter than twelve feet; this, with a line from one to one and a half times the length of the rod, is sufficient to keep the angler out of sight in the clearest water.

And with respect to the reel line, the one you use for fly-fishing will suit the purpose. That for casting should be fine, long, and well tapered; the lower portions composed of four lengths of the *very finest gut* that can be had, tinged with the ordinary decoction of logwood and copperas.

As to the size of hook best adapted for this mode of fishing, I recommend James Dyson's round bend No. 6, fine wire, which can be purchased of Mr Thompson, fishing-tackle manufacturer, Hexham. In attaching worm hooks to the gut, use fine silk thread of a crimson colour. See that it be well waxed, and adopt a small projection of gut or bristle to keep the worm in position, so as to prevent it from slipping down and exposing the shank of the hook; then carefully lap downwards, and finish with two hitch knots;—a touch of spirit varnish makes all secure.

Many different kinds of worms are used by the angler; but above all others I prefer the moss-worm, which, unfortunately, is very scarce, and to be found only in certain localities. Although around Aid Crag, the vicinity of Woodburn, and other places where the ground is of a mossy nature, they may be had. they may also be obtained among old clots or sods by the sides of open drains. When taken from the earth they are of a creamy hue, and on being kept a few days, and put through the process of toughening, subsequently recommended, they assume a lively pink colour. Next to the moss-worm ranks the brandling, which species of worm is too well-known to require any description, as it is to be found around nearly every farm-steading, and is a good substitute for the moss-worm when the latter cannot be procured.

A small bright lively worm is always more enticing to a well fed trout than a big soft reptile; and when the waters are clear worms can hardly be had too small, if they will cover the hook. A worm from two to three inches long, and about the thickness of a hen quil, is the largest size that should be used.

Worms on being unearthed (and not intended for immediate use,) should be placed for three or four minutes in a vessel containing water; the farther effect of this immersion is to cleanse them partially of what imparts to the skin a dingy hue. Thus washed, they should be allowed to crawl about on a clean dry board, with a view of freeing them from all superfluous moisture. When this is sufficiently done, transfer them into a large jar, filled, or nearly so, with hartshorn moss.

The hartshorn is a species of moss found chiefly on moorland and in boggy places surrounded by heath. Externally, on the exposed parts, it possesses a reddish tinge; the lower foliage is of a pale yellow. When dry it keeps for years, and the worm-fisher ought to possess a stock of it, as in cultivated districts it is difficult to procure. Before using the moss, let it be well washed, the hard and whitish stalks twitched off, and the red portions retained. The drier the moss among which the worms are placed, the quicker they become fit for use; at the same time be it remembered, their natural juices are sooner exhausted, and if kept beyond a certain period without moisture, pine away and die.

The dryness of the moss ought, therefore, to be regulated by circumstances — by the state of the weather, the temperature of the apartment where the jar is placed, and the time its contents are required to be used.

The essential matter is to have your worms red and lively. This can be accomplished by feeding them on a species of highly coloured earth, reduced to a fine powder resembling brick dust. This may be purchased at any druggist's, under the name of Bole Armenian. Being deprived of their natural sustenance in the shape of earth, the worms consume a portion of it as their food, imbibing at the same time its alluring colour. It is administered to them by being first moistened with water, then mixed among the moss. While undergoing the above mentioned process, they should be placed in a cool shady place.

Regarding the time of day when trout take most greedily, that depends not a little on the state of the atmosphere. In warm weather they are in feeding humour shortly after sunrise, and continue to be so until one or two p.m.; generally, however, they do not take freely before eight or nine a.m. The whole of a pool may be fished when there is a breeze upon it. When there is no wind, the only part of a pool worth fishing is the strong rush at the head. But the streams are what the angler should rely upon; and the best trout are to be got in shallow water, close on the edge of the strong run.

In trouting with the worm in clear waters, all able anglers cast up stream. Angling up stream with the worm possesses all the advantages which have been mentioned in fly-fishing; and to fish up a clear water, a proper casting of the line is of primary importance. The two things to be attended to are—first, to throw highly, so as not to break the worm; and secondly, to throw with certainty to any required spot. In casting a worm, you should allow it to go out behind, then urge it forward slowly; all sudden jerks must be avoided, as they are apt to tear the worm. The point of the rod should go nearer the water than in casting a fly; and extend the rod to the full length, in order to get the bait as far out as possible. In doing this you must not lower the point of the rod till you have given the worm all the forward impetus intended; then lower it slowly almost to a level with the water, and the worm will go to the full stretch of both rod and line. Whenever the worm alights, raise your rod gradually, but take care not to raise it so quickly as in any way to interfere with the motion of the worm. It is of great importance that there should be very little line in the water, not so much because it is calculated to alarm the trout, as that the action of the stream upon the line will in some cases bring the worm much faster down than it would otherwise come; in others it will bring it nearer the surface, and in either case giving an unnatural motion to the lure. As already remarked, all able worm fishers invariably cast up stream; in so doing they take up their stand below where the trout are presumed to lie, never allowing the bait as it is carried down to pass below them. This practice embodies two advantages, both of which demand attention. In the first place, he is kept better concealed from the wary eye of the trout, which, as is well known, when resting fronts the current, and, although possessed of visual organs sufficiently prominent to detect objects above or on either side, can descry but very partially what takes place in its rear; and secondly, from his position he can strike with greater certainty and effect. In this particular he acquires a very decided advantage over the old fangled mode of worm-fishing, that, namely, of casting down stream, adopting which system the angler, when striking, is more apt to pull the hook fairly out of the mouth of the fish without even pricking it, than when he throws against the current and strikes downwards to bring the bend and barb in contact with the mouth of the trout. A third advantage obtained by the mode of casting recommended is that the water is less disturbed, the unavoidable plunging of the wader affecting only those portions of the water that lie below him. The other advice conveyed by the practice, never allow the bait which is carried down by the current to pass below you, lift it always before coming in line with the opposite bank of the river. In permitting it to descend farther you not only angle without much hope of success, but you frighten more good trout than you are aware of. A fish, for instance, has just caught a glimpse of your bait as it travels towards you; he follows it, but by the time he can give you any intimation of his approach it is carried down either to your feet or to a short distance on either side of where you stand. Still he pursues it, but being made aware of your presence he becomes alarmed, darts off, and scares all the fish in that place; whereas, had you lifted your worm in sufficient time you would have left him above you on the look out, and readier than ever to seize the bait when again thrown beyond him. The first notice you get of a trout having taken your lure is a stoppage of the line. This is the moment for striking, as in clear water fishing the greatest error that the angler can fall into is to feel for the trout. Never do this, but on the least tug at your lure or straightening of your line—*strike*. In performing the movement, do so steadily, and with firmness, not by means of a jerk, which is apt either to snap the gut or tear away the hold obtained by the hook; and remember always to strike downwards, or as near as possible with the flow of the stream. In playing a trout, let out as little line as possible, and never allow it to get slack. In taking the fish out of the water, take him out with your hands; never attempt to lift him with the line, or you are almost sure to lose both your trout and your temper.

THE WANSBECK AND COQUET.—These rivers have been frequently in a state of spate of late, and angling has been uncertain. Some good sport has, however, been frequently met with, and a Newcastle angler sends me word that several good baskets of trout have been caught lately. Mr James Armstrong, well known as an angler, otter hunter, and breeder of Dandie Dinmonts, has been as successful perhaps as any one, and he has captured some very nice trout in both streams with a bait that is said to be a very attractive one to the trout in general, and in this district particularly, viz, the mossworm; in four days Mr Armstrong captured 68lb. of trout with it, viz, 18lb. in the Wansbeck on June 10, 16lb on the 11th, and 19lb on the 13th; and on the 20th he basketed 15lb in the Coquet.—J. E. M. From "The Field" of the 12th of July, 1879.

ON FISHING WITH THE MINNOW FOR TROUT.

In handling this subject, I shall briefly lay before the reader a summary of useful information which, if carried out, will be found to be one of the most deadly methods of fishing with the minnow for trout.

The largest trout taken by the rod are caught by the minnow. Trout accustomed to prey upon their neighbours attain great size, and may be more readily taken by the minnow than by any other means. Minnows are not easily caught, however, and a great many contrivances are used to capture them, but the most reliable of all the methods yet employed for the purpose is the "minnow trap," which can be purchased of almost any fishing-tackle manufacturer, who will give you full instructions how to use it, but at first glance that is easily seen, and what has been held to be the secret of preserving minnows is simply this: As soon as you catch your minnows put them among the *best malt whisky*, when they will be fit either for immediate use, or keep firm for years.

A minnow measuring about an inch and three quarters (tail included) is the best size, and always select the best shaped and silvery coloured ones, those of a greenish colour are worthless. As regards the rod, this should be fifteen feet long, and stiff.

The reel line in common use will answer very well for this also. The casting line should be triple spun, and three feet long, to which add six lengths of good round clean gut. And as regards hooks, I have tried all kinds, and experience teaches me that two hooks, with a drag behind, will kill more than any other combination. Take a small sized salmon hook and tie it on to your lowest length of gut; then take a worm hook (No 5) and tie it on close above the salmon hook, so that the bend of the small hook may just touch the shank end of the large one.

The drag consists of triple hooks tied on to a separate length of gut, with a loop at one end to slip on above the shank end of No. 5 hook. The drag, I may remark, should, when stretched out, be three and a half inches behind the minnow; the tail of which, in spinning, describes a ring as it were, and the drag being still farther out catch the trout that bite shy or miss the minnow.

With regard to swivels, one should be placed two feet above the hooks, and a second two feet and a half farther up. Two or three split shot (No. 3) should be placed between the swivels, varying them according to circumstances in heavy water, more if necessary.

In attaching the minnow, enter the large hook at the mouth, and run the fish in the same manner as you would a worm along over the bend and shank. When about a quarter of an inch from the tail bring through the barb, allowing it to protrude freely, then thrust the smaller hook through the lips of the minnow to keep it in position.

Trout take the minnow most readily when the water is just beginning to rise; then it is that the trout leave the banks and stones where they have been keeping out of sight when the waters were small and clear. When the water is in full flood little can be done, but when it is beginning to subside the trout will again take the minnow greedily, the tails of streams and sides of pools are the spots you should then fish for them. Trout take the minnow more in June and July than at any other time of the season, and, if the weather be rough, a flooded water in these months is a certain sign of sport.

As to the proper mode of playing or working the minnow I require to say little. It should be subjected, in fact, to every variety of *movement*. Sometimes it ought to be urged along with short measured jerks ; sometimes drawn steadily against the stream in one continued pull ; in short, there is no possible mode of playing this lure which may not prove successful in attracting trout, and, remember, never lift your minnow till it is close to the edge.

A trout when fairly on the feed makes a grand rush at a minnow; this is the time to be cool, and slacken your line for four or five seconds or so, *then strike* full and firm, and in four cases out of five your fish will be hooked.

When the weather is warm, and the streams small and clear, trout will take the minnow all night ; the fish then feed in the shallow water at the foot of pools, and at such times I have known *keen anglers* capture many a good creel of yellow-fins.

THE CURING OF SALMON ROE, AND HOW TO FISH WITH IT.

(Chiefly extracted from Stoddart's Angler's Companion.)

There are two or three **ways of curing salmon roe**. It is either cured entire—that is, as it is taken from the fish in the form of what is provincially termed the "waim"; or it is reduced into a paste; or else it is converted to single particles termed beads.

The first object of the curer is to obtain what is reckoned an available supply of roe. Much of the ingredient met with under that name is next to useless, the seed or ova being too small in the particle, or else through an injury done to the fish from which they are taken, largely transfused with blood. In either case, and under other circumstances easily recognisable, it ought to be rejected. The roe best adapted for curing is to be found in the " baggit " fish. or ripe spawner; that is, a salmon on the eve of depositing its ova. The beads or pellets should, unless intended to be cured in the way first mentioned,—have attained their full size, equalling that of a small pea or swan shot. They ought, moreover, to be distinct and easily separated, as well as of a high pink or brick colour.

In every preparation of this bait, the first step of the process is to cleanse the leaf, by removing from it the clotted blood and other impurities which it may happen to have contracted. In some cases, when the roe is designed to be cured in the leaf, this may be done simply with a cloth or towel; the natural juices are thus kept intact in their primitive condition. But it seldom happens that the leaf is so pure and undamaged as to allow of such a superficial mode of cleansing. Accordingly, in most cases, it is found essential to wash and pick it. To do this properly use water slightly warmed and mixed with a small quantity of milk. Perform the operation in a large hand-basin, and transfer, when cleansed, each leaf, layer, or fragment, to a sieve or cullender, by means of which the superfluous fluid will most readily be drained off. Thus cleansed and strained, the roe is made fit for one or other of the processes of curing already alluded to.

The speediest and most efficacious method of curing the roe for immediate use is this: Take the layers of roe as they are taken from the fish, cleanse them from all adhering particles of blood, then take a piece of flannel, and after spreading it out on a table, place upon it one of the layers, sprinkle it thoroughly with salt, roll once or twice round with the flannel, then proceed in a like manner with the next, and so on, until the flannel is full; expose the whole then to a gentle heat. In the course of two or three hours it will have become firm and of a most glutinous nature, in which state it is ready for use.

In curing roe in the leaf, saltpetre is sometimes employed with a view of heightening its colour. I would recommend, however, that this ingredient be used very sparingly, as its flavour is by no means palatable to the fish, nor indeed are its effects in improving the natural colour of the bait otherwise than doubtful.

There are two modes of preparing paste from the salmon roe. The one generally adopted is the least tedious, and although the ingredient produced from it is not so equal or thoroughly broken up or mixed as that of the other, it possesses all, and to spare, of its attractive virtues, being a compound of the bead and paste, and on this account insinuating itself into the good graces of the bull-trout, which species of fish give a preference to unbroken over finely reduced roe. The following is the method to be observed in preparing it: After cleansing, proceed to break down the leaf, separating at the same time the beads and pellets from the films to which they are attached, then throw over them a quantity of fine salt in the proportion of three or four ounces or upwards to every pound of roe, and stirring the mixture with the hand, incorporate all thoroughly, also squeeze together, and occasion to burst several handfuls of the beads, in order that, thus expressed, their adhesive contents may operate in binding and giving consistency to those left intact. This process concluded, transfer the whole mass to a tin cullender, there to remain under cover for some hours, during which time a considerable quantity of oily matter becomes separated and drained off, the pieces of the pellets being acted upon by the salt to this effect. When the draining has ceased, the paste is ready for use. If intended to be kept for some time, remove it into small pots, pressing it well down with the hand in filling, and running over it a little melted lard.

The other preparation of roe-paste alluded to undergoes up to a certain stage the same process as the one above described. After the beads, however, have been separated, place them in a jug or deep jar, and by means of a small wooden shaft or pestle, bruise, mix, and stir them up vigorously, until every individual pellet has become broken and dissolved, and the whole forms a thick, creamy-looking substance. During this operation, which is somewhat of a tedious one, and will occupy the person engaged in it at least an hour, a handful of salt ought from time to time to be added. When all has been thoroughly incorporated and mixed up together, pour boiling water upon the mass and it will instantly harden and become formed into a solid lump of paste, capable of being removed by the hand. The water, be it again remarked, must be quite hot, and poured into the jug or basin containing the roe, not applied to it externally. This is the true secret of preparing salmon-roe paste.

Of the curing of this ingredient in the bead state, little is required to be said. It consists simply in the drying and packing up of the roe in the separated pellets, and requires no process beyond that of submitting them to the action of air and heat until sufficiently toughened, and then committing them to earthenware pots or small jars.

In curing salmon roe for bait, the preservation of its natural colour should always be kept in view. The sweetness of taste also is a matter upon which some anglers lay great stress. If by that is meant freedom in the flavour of the roe from salt, I take the liberty of differing with them; for there is no doubt that, independent of the properties of the roe itself, that substance possesses qualities of its own highly attractive in their nature. These, in regard to wild animals of various kinds, are well known;

they are exemplified in the instance of what is termed by the American hunter*—" a salt lick," or moist spot of ground highly impregnated with the mineral in question. To this, deer and game of all descriptions repair from great distances, lured by the attractive nature of the salt. I am of opinion, therefore, that the flavour of this substance is very agreeable to trout, in common with other animals, and that a measure of the success met with by the angler in fishing with salmon roe is owing to its liberal use.

I shall now very briefly direct the attention of the reader to the tackle best adapted for roe-fishing, interspersing a few instructions as to the proper mode of angling with this attractive and deadly bait. The hooks to be used are No. 7, two of which tie back to back, and press forward by means of the finger and thumb, so as to be at right angles with each other. These serve sufficiently to retain or secure the bait, without resorting to wool or cotton fibres. Leaf roe I seldom fish with, preferring the mixed paste already described. I also employ strong round gut, and weight or lead my line largely, in order to keep the bait from progressing too rapidly.

In fishing with the salmon roe, I recommend the following instructions : Let the angler be provided

*See Stoddart's "Angler's Companion."

with a stiffish single-handed rod, and the tackle already described; sally forth either alone or consorted, at most with one companion; he may then betake himself to a favourable stretch of water, the depth being from two to five feet, the bottom gravelly and free from impediments, and the current gradual. Near the head of this he ought to select his stand, on a dry and unexposed portion of the bank. There is no necessity on commencing operations that he should bait the spot; this in the course of a few throws will be done sufficiently. In throwing, the angler should generally employ a short line, not much exceeding his rod in length, and occasionally a good deal shorter. He can always in that highly discoloured state of the water, in which salmon roe is most effective as a bait, entice his spoil to within a yard's distance from the margin. Accordingly, he loses no advantage by employing the description of line recommended; and in the matter of striking, acquires a very important one. Sometimes, however, in certain localities, and when bull-trout are on the feed, it may be expedient to increase the length of his cast or throw; also in brown or fine waters it is essential to do so.

In baiting with the mixed or other paste, let the angler extract a small portion, equal in size to a horse bean, from the pot or jar. This may be done readily, by means of an old pocket-knife, or other sharp-pointed instrument. He then requires to insert the bait in question betwixt the projecting barbs of his hooks, in the angle formed by their junction. A slight pressure of the forefinger will assist greatly in attaching it; but it is not necessary to conceal every portion of the wire, as in worm-fishing. When casting, the angler ought to be extremely cautious, lest by excess of force he should occasion his bait to drop off. He will find it preferable to pitch it out gently from him, instead of throwing the line over his shoulder; this in general he requires to do partially up and against the stream, not forward at right angles with the bank, as is practised under the ordinary style of roe-fishing. He must then allow the bait to sink rapidly, and to travel at a measured rate along the bottom or channel. When checked, he ought to consider it seized by a fish, and on such occasions to act as if it were so, striking down in the direction of the current.

In the mode of fishing recommended, the angler, as already hinted, should restrict his operations to a single spot in the range or beat occupied by him; doing so, he will most effectually concentrate the feeding trout. He should on all occasions keep his line *taut*, sounding as it were the bottom with the leads attached to it, and holding on the alert, in case of any sudden strain or stoppage arising from the interference of a fish with his bait. On favourable days this will happen in the course of every cast or throw taken by him, and he has only to strike at the proper moment to secure the trout. March, April, October, and November being unquestionably the most suitable months, a flooded river during one or other of them is the sure index of sport. The proper moment for commencing operations is when the water on its decrease has begun to assume a yellow or light brown appearance, the particles of sand and soil being still, to some extent, in an unsettled state. From this period until the water merges into the deepest brown or black colour, the salmon roe may be successfully fished with, as it is the most attractive and deadly bait that can be employed in capturing trout.

HOW TO COOK A TROUT AT THE RIVER SIDE.

Kindle a fire of dry wood; take your fish when just out of the water, or from your creel, roll him up in some damp clay, then lay the fish among the embers of your fire; when the clay presents a white colour, which generally occurs when it has got thoroughly hard and cracked, the trout is properly done, and a slight blow will easily remove the clay, and display to the hungry angler a delicious meal. Wandering tribes of gipsies frequently may be seen cooking various dishes in the above manner. The fish, I may observe, must not be cut open and cleaned. During the firing process the intestines and other impurities will draw together, and not in the slightest degree injure the trout. In the absence of clay, paper may be used. Two or three folds of old newspapers rolled round the fish, the ends being twisted together, the whole then completely soaked in water and placed on the fire until well charred, will answer the same purpose. Salt will improve the flavour of your trout.

To the Fishing Away.

O joyfu' the lark spreads his wee dewy wings,
An' far in the blue skies sae sweetly he sings;
The curlew an' pliver wing their way to the west,
To the mosses an' flowes, and the knowes they like
    best.
The flow'rets are springing in clusters, my lad;
The throssels are singing sae blithesome and glad;
Our hearts are sae lightsome, a' nature sae gay,
We'll off to the streams, to the fishing away.

The cuckoo an' swallow ance mair they return,
An' the wee water-waggie's away up the burn,
On the bough o' the hazel the tassels they hing,
On the brink o' the streamlet the primroses spring,
The gorcock craws crouse on the mossie grey stane,
The blackcock croos proud round his bonnie grey
    hen;
At the first peep o' morn in the sun's early ray
We'll off to the streams, to the fishing away.

Wi' gad, creel, an' tackle, wi' mossbait an' flee,
We'll ower the heather sae gladsome and free,
An' doun by the linns where the dun otters hide,
And fish the clear streams where the yellow trouts
    glide.

We'll ramble the Kielder an' Coquet sae fine,
The Reed, Jed, and Liddel, and bonnie North Tyne;
We'll fling up our bonnets, an' gie a hurray,
An' off to the streams, to the fishing away.

DANDIE DINMONT AND HIS TERRIERS.

Respecting James Davidson, of Hindlee, and his dogs, old Watty Jackson of Catcleuch gives much valuable information. "Monie a time," says that veteran hunter, "hae I huntit wi' Jamie; an' frae what Sir Walter reytes aboot Dandie Dinmont an' his Pepper an' Mustard terriers, Jamie was the verra man, there's nae doot o't; for his terriers wer maistly Peppers an' Mustards, —lang backit, shurt leggit customers; maybe rather shurt i' the leg for rinnin' efter the huns ower rough grun; but Jamie was up to that; he aye carryit twae o' them in a wallet, ane on eyther seyde, afore him on the galloway's back; an' when the fox holed, they wer fresh. I mind yence o' my faither an' him howkin ane at the Little Worchet yonder; an' the fox gat Jamie by the han' an' he shoots 'Ha! the lim', he's beyten!

Aweel, aweel my frien,' quoth Jamie, 'if ye'll keep yer grip, I'll keep mine!' Od; I could tell ye ower as monie o' Jamie's brecks as wad fill a hale beuik."

But to Dr Grant, of Hawick, I am mostly indebted for my information on this celebrated race of dogs, he being recognised as the best judge in Britain; and I may state that, should ever that learned gentleman feel inclined to publish the voluminous manuscripts in his possession regarding the above, it would tend greatly to enlighten the public as to the interpretation of that celebrated novelist, Sir Walter Scott. On the authority of the Doctor, therefore, I give the various

Points and Characteristics of a Pure and Perfect Dandie Dinmont Terrier.

Head: Large and long, with very strong jaws, and teeth which are quite level; the head of the bitch is generally smaller than that of the dog. Ears: From three to four inches long. They should not be round at the point and broad like the hound, but somewhat in shape of the almond or filbert. No doubt the close lying ears look best, but it is not essential that either one or both ears should lie flat. Many of the best bred Dandies

I have seen, when they were in much greater abundance on the Borders, carried one or both ears somewhat up, and I never met with the peculiarity in any but a thoroughly game animal. Like Sir Walter Scott, I prefer the small triangular ear, whether it lie flat or not, provided it be set properly on to lie well back, so as to be as far as possible out of the way of punishment in battle when closing with fox or otter. Nose: A flesh-coloured nose in a reddish coloured Dandie is not objectionable, and does not in any way constitute him an illegitimate member of the Dinmont family; but I like the black nose best for Dandies of every colour. Eyes: Full, bright, and intelligent. The colour may vary much, and is, like the colour of the claws, fixed by mere influence of nature, that regulate the colour of the animal's coat. The "hazel" colour in all its shades I like most, and the darker it is so as to appear black when in its deepest hue, pleases my taste best. Neck: Well developed and rather short. Body: Long, with low shoulders and the back slightly curved down behind them, with a corresponding arch of the loin. Legs: Short, particularly in front, and turned out at the toes, with extraordinary strength of bone and muscle, in proportion to the animal's size. Tail: Somewhat curved, and carried over the back, with more or less feather, or almost none in some instances. Height: From about 10 to 13 inches at top of shoulder. Coat: A mixture of hardish and soft short hair, with more or less of silky hair of a lighter colour on the head, the legs and feet partaking to a slight extent of the same. Colour: Either reddish brown or bluish grey, or a combination of both, in which case part of the body and back is bluish grey, while the legs, and sometimes a large portion, if not the entire head, inside of ears, chest, and underside of tail is reddish brown, or verging on a pale tan or fawn colour. Weight: From 13 to 22lbs. Claws: White claws I positively object to as being proof of in-and-in-breeding, though it is not proof in itself of impurity. Yellow claws are natural to reddish brown and flaxen-coloured Dandies, and are, therefore, not objectionable; while jet black claws on those light-coloured dogs are, like black eyes and black noses, by far the greatest beauty spots of the Dandie Dinmont race.

The following is the

Genealogy of the Dandie Dinmont Terriers belonging to Dr. Grant, of Hawick,

whose far-famed kennel of Dandies are by "THE DRUID," and other sporting writers, allowed to rank among the foremost in the canine peerage of the world.

Dr. Grant's (dogs) "Tom" and "Piper," by his "Shamrock III." and out of his "Nettle." "Shamrock III." by "Pepper III.," belonging to Sir George H. S. Douglas, of Springwood Park, Kelso, by his "Pepper II." "Pepper II." by his "Pepper I." Pepper I." was by "Dandie II." belonging to Mr. John Stoddart of Selkirk, by his "Dandie I." "Dandie I." was out of a bitch named "Gypp," belonging to the late James Davidson of Hindlee.

The dam of "Shamrock III." was a bitch named "Vixen," belonging to James Scott, by his "Shamrock II. "Shamrock II." was by Mr Brisbane's "Dandie," bred by Lord Elcho. Dr. Grant's "Nettle," the dam of "Tom" and "Piper" was by his "Black Jack," and out of his "Gypp II." "Gypp II." by his "Glorious Jack," and out of his "Lucy Anne." "Lucy Anne" out of "Muss." "Muss" out of "Vic." "Vic" out of "Maida. "Maida" out of "Meadow," (the renowned terrier bitch referred to in a book entitled *Stonehenge on the Dog*. See page 78.) "Meadow" by a dog named "Pepper," belonging to Sir George H. S. Douglas, and out of his "Schann." "Schann" by his "Old Pepper." "Old Pepper" was by "Dandie I." "Dandie I." was out of "Gypp," (the bitch already referred to) belonging the late James Davidson of Hindlee.

The above genealogy I extracted from the Dandie Dinmont records in the possession of Dr. Grant; and may observe that Ned Dunn, of White Lea; Davie Kyle, of Broadlee; Yeddie Jackson, of Fairloans; Tom Potts, of Burnmouth; the Telfers of Skaap, and the Telfers of Blindburn,* were in possession of terriers that were sprung from those of the "Pepper" and "Mustard" breed possessed by James Davidson.

* The Telfers of Blindburn, nephews of Dandie Dinmont.

DESCRIPTION OF OTTER HUNTING IN THE TEVIOT.

OTTER hunting is unquestionably one of our best national amusements, and the most exciting of all our field sports. One of the most brilliant and dashing hunts of the sort ever witnessed in the borders of Scotland occurred on Friday morning, May 29, 1863, in the Teviot, with Dr. Grant's otter hounds, and has since been the theme of conversation among all classes of society in the district. The hunt was well supported, and among the many present on foot as well as on horseback we observed the Hon. Arthur Elliot, Colonel Elliot (brother of the Right Hon. the Earl of Minto), the Hon. Wm. Fitzwilliam Elliot, William Rodgie, Esq., Alfred Wilson, Esq., Robert Selby, Esq., W. B. Graham, Esq., &c., &c. The hounds were thrown off at 6 a.m. below Burnfoot, and from the beginning all could see that the Doctor was at work in real earnest. Among the rocks in the river below Hornshole, Caledonia first challenged the drag, and, well supported by her companions, Royal, Ringwood, and Pibroch, ran it briskly to above Teviotbank, where it was lost. For reasons only known (so far as we are aware) to the huntsman and his special friends, some of whom had been out all the night by the river side stopping drains and making observations, no time was put off here in searching for the otter's whereabouts; but off they dashed to opposite Minto, where the river runs deep, and the bank on the south side is densely wooded, very steep, and its margin extensively excavated below every here and there, owing to the river during the floods washing away the sandy soil from among the roots of the sturdy trees. The Doctor having first rid himself of his horse, cheered his hounds to the river and sent them across. Some took to dragging the land, while the brave and renowned Ringwood preferred swimming down the river, smelling every stone, hole, and cranny as he passed it. All were quiet, eagerly viewing with admiration the instinct of the dogs, when Ringwood broke silence by a hearty burst of music which told its own tale, while he "set" an otter far away underground beneath an elm tree, and wrought his way eagerly through the dense network of the roots into his halt, where he fought the first of single-handed subterranean conflicts that followed. Up came the other hounds quickly, with raised hackles and their sterns up. In dashed the wise old Royal to support his friend. The other hounds cheered them with the most vociferous bursts of music from above, while their master called out "Hark to Ringwood and Royal. Mark him, good old hounds. Ho! go at him! Yoicks!" The otter slipped away, and was viewed by Broadwith, Stoddart, and several others, swimming cleverly up the river under water. Stoddart sung out "Here he goes, Doctor; he is a big one; now for sport!" However, he gained one of his strongholds from below water, and into which no hole could be found. A messenger was despatched to Deanfoot to bring picks and spades, Caledonia having marked him far back several feet below the surface of the bank. A hole was being made there to insert the terrier, when the otter voluntarily shifted ground; but no sooner had he done so than he gained another place of shelter of the same sort farther down, and also without any entry from above. Here again he was marked far back from the river, and another hole required to be dug over him to admit a dog. He slipped away there, and endeavoured to cross the country to the Rule. The hounds seemed alive to his movements, were soon on his track, overshot him, and headed him back to the Teviot, when he was viewed down the bank by one of Lord Minto's sons, and tallyhoed into the river. For a while after he seemed lost, and a friend remarked to the huntsman that it would be impossible to make anything of him, and strongly advised him to draw off the hounds. "By no means, while we are able to work and the hounds to hunt," was the reply of the Doctor, whom energy and perseverance have so strongly characterised all his lifetime. At this moment Mr Broadwith's celebrated dog Slash made a desperate dash under water, and gained a shelf of the beach underground, where he discovered the game and had a desperate encounter with him. But the otter escaped somehow or other from the powerful jaws of Slash, who came out after him showing the *crimson* in different places, especially about the ears. Ever afterwards he was so incessantly tormented by the persuasive eloquence of the hounds at one time, and the application of their ivory at another, to keep moving for his own sake, that he constantly shifted ground, dodging up and down from one halt to another with his enemies closely pursuing him. In the end he broke away over Spittalford, a considerable way down the river. Mr Stoddart viewed him, gave the alarm, and stuck closely to him with his dog.

The Doctor with a whoop of his horn instantly gathered the hounds, bounded into the saddle with a loud tally-ho, and galloped at a dangerous pace along the beach and through the very channel of the river below the ford till he reached the new field of action. On seeing the game dog contending bravely with the otter, though much distressed and at the risk of being drowned, for the otter had decidedly the best of it, he jumped from his horse, dashed into the river, and fearlessly caught the brute by the tail under water with an amount of dexterity that will long be remembered by those who saw the feat, and at once brought the savage creature to bay. By this time, however, the Doctor was much fatigued, and required even to be supported by Stoddart and others, while they dragged him by his own urgent request from the river across the beach along with the otter and dog still entangled in lively combat. He unfortunately fell on his back at the time, but no admonition could prevail on him to quit the otter's tail. The hounds by this time were up, and the Doctor asked assistance to take them all back that he might have the honour of introducing to the otter a pet terrier that had never had the pleasure of meeting an otter before. It was led by a chain with a collar round its neck. He brought him forward and allowed the *varmint* to bite his cheek, saying " Go at him Bobby." To everybody's surprise, Bobby was in no way discomposed, but turned his face coolly to his adversary without a whimper, and in a few seconds was locked in the otter's throat by his jaws, and he never shifted his hold till he completed his work, and was removed by the hand of his masters. All the dogs were then allowed to gratify themselves by tattering the dead carcass in return for the many compliments it had paid them during the hunt, which had lasted over three hours and a half. The Doctor became faint from over-exertion, and through such had to throw himself down for a little on the cold ground. The otter was a male, and aged, weighing 25 lbs., and measuring $50\frac{1}{4}$ inches in length. A word here may not be out of place regarding the master and his hounds. Dr Grant is a native of Strathspey in the Highlands of Scotland, where his forefathers constituted a powerful and a warlike clan more than six hundred years ago. He is a *thorough-bred* clansman, and the representative of the eighteenth branch of the " Honourable family of Grant of Grant," being the fifth descendant of Patrick, second son of James Laird, of Grant, who founded the family of Wester Elchies in 1663 (see " Shaw's History of Moray; or the Genealogy of the Grant

Family") and through life he has stamped himself a deserving representative of his family; a gentleman, and a true-hearted sportsman. He is one of those who advocate fair play to the otter as strenuously as he advocates fair play to the hound, believing the pleasure of the chase to be more in the *pursuit* than in the *death* of the game, and those who know him will never envy the position of those who may inadvertently tamper unfairly either with the otter or with the hound. The beautiful condition of the hounds, their highly-developed instinct, their thorough gameness, and exquisite training, coupled with the frank deportment of their unassuming, though accomplished leader, are attractions of no ordinary nature, and render it a matter of no surprise that the nobility and gentry of the district so thoroughly enjoy a morning's recreation with them by the river side.

FOXHUNTING IN THE REEDWATER COUNTRY.

The morning after the football match at Horsley a joyous party of foxhunters met the Border foxhounds on the heights of Catcleugh. We are early afoot, and have a fine view of many a hill and glen which of old was the haunt of the wolf and red deer and the rugged retreat of the fierce reebooter. Yonder come the hounds, and in their wake are the mounted hunters, twelve in number, among whom are the two Miss Robson's of Byrness, and Miss Dodd of the Leam, all three ardent followers of the foxhunt on the mountains, and true votaries of the goddess of the silver bow. The hounds are cast around all the likely ground for a drag but without success, till they wind round the watershed between Coquet and Reed, and on Thirlmoor the sweet notes of the beauties proclaim that bold reynard has been on the wander. We are out of the hunt, however, unless fortune favours us, as we are far in the rear on Raven Knowe, in company with T. Robson, a herd callant, and R. Oliver, a firm and wiry foxhunter, whose keen eye marks the line of the dogs as they are streaming away for Cankercleugh. Ha! yonder's a check, and a cast. Now they are on again, and over the edge for Coquet, straight in a line for Cheviot. Hurrah! they sweep round, yonder they come along the Herden Edge. We are in for a hunt yet; the fox means the Reedwater country, after all noo watch alang the weather gleam for the fox, says our friend with the falcon eye, ye may ken by yon curlew that he's no far off; see, yon's him. And we get a momentary glimpse of something between us and the snow on the peak of Cheviot. Aye, faix it's him; here he comes straight to us. Noo jouk down an' let him past. Whisht! there he is wi' his tongue oot; he's gae hard up already. He's past the holes at the Raven Crag, the hounds close on him, Bellman leading, all giving tongue fit to waken the fairies at the Whurlstone. And here come three of the riders, young Elliot of Hindhope first, a Dandie Dinmont of Blindburn next, and close up Miss E. Robson of Byrness, the fair haired sister of the gallant young master of the pack. There's huntin' bluid for ye, exclaimed our friend of Speethope Haugh, as the young lady dashed past, and whose brilliant illustration of horsewomanship forcibly reminds us of the incident of a hunting excursion when the steed of her sire lost its shoes in that desperate foxhunt on the Cheviots. A wild hallo we now hear in the distance. The fox is holed at the Saughy Crag. The terrier is in when we get forward, the fox has been too hard run to bolt for fun, but after two hours towzling he at last slips out and up the crag, along the height, chops back, and doubles like a hare, then over the braes through the firs past Cottonshope Burn foot, the gallant pack sticking to their fox like a brother, and again run him to ground on Saughside, where he has scarce room to hide, and we see some grand battles in turns with my nabs and the terriers, the game little "Rock" (belonging to that gallant sportsman, Mr William Hedley, of Cottenshope Burn) gets a good snedding, so does Flint, the celebrated terrier of the Byrness; the dog of Speethope Haugh has a long tug, too, but the weaver gets a gliff and turns tail. In a twinkling the fox bolts and on to the side of the Reed, the dogs on him full cry. See yon black and tan, he's gaining on him every stride, there is a rush of fox and hounds over the brae into the water. It's a kill; no, by Jove, it's a fair otter hunt. The fox is out, so are the hounds. Wellington is at him, and tumbles up his game. The various incidents of this brilliant run were witnessed by the author, and at the request of several of our Border foxhunters I here give it as a reprint.

THE BEDLINGTON TERRIER.

Owing to the public interest that has long attached, and still does attach, to the above interesting breed of dogs, I believe the following exhaustive account of this dog-fanciers' pet will be acceptable.

HISTORY OF THE BREED.

To make the matter clearly understood, it may be necessary to premise that during the first quarter of the present century, Mr Edward Donkin, of Flotterton—still dear to the old sportsmen of Coquetside by the familiar soubriquet of "Hunting Ned"—hunted a pack of foxhounds well known in the Rothbury district. At that time he possessed two very celebrated kennel terriers, "Peachem" and "Pincher," which are alluded to in the pedigree below. A colony of sporting nailers then flourished at Bedlington, who were noted for their plucky breed of terriers. But reform was at hand, and the old favourites were obliged to make way for new blood. To Joseph Ainsley, a mason by trade, belongs this honour. He purchased a dog named "Peachem," of a Mr Wm. Cowen, of Rothbury, and the result of a union of this dog with Mr Christopher Dixon's "Phœbe," of Longhorsley, was "Piper," belonging James Anderson, of Rothbury Forest. Piper was a dog of slender build, about 15 inches high, and 15lb weight. He was of a liver colour, the hair being a sort of hard woolly lint, his ears were large, hung close to his cheek, and were slightly feathered at the tip.

In the year 1820, Mr J. Howe, of Alnwick, visited a friend at Bedlington, and brought with him a terrier bitch, named Phœbe, which he left with Mr Edward Coates, of the Vicarage. Phœbe belonged to Mr Andrew Riddell, of Framlington, who subsequently made a present of her to Ainsley, but from the fact of her home being at the Vicarage, she was generally known as "Coates's Phœbe." Her colour was black or black blue, and she had the invariable light coloured silky tuft on her head. She was about thirteen inches high, and weighed 14lbs. In 1825 she was mated with Anderson's Piper, and the fruit of this union was the Bedlington terrier in question. Of the sagacity and courage of Ainsley's Piper, one of their offspring, a volume might be written, and to submit a list of the best known specimens would be tedious. There were Ainsley's Ranter (of Redheugh, Gateshead), Coates's Peachem, Weatherburn's Phœbe, Hoy's Rocky, Fish's Crib, and, in short, a host of tried ones.

The old and true breed is now scarce, and there are few indeed, even in Northumberland, able to furnish a reliable pedigree of the original doughty specimen. In some instances the cross with the otter hound has been indulged in, but the result was disappointment. The bull strain introduced, it is supposed, for fighting purposes; and for rabbit coursing, the leggy beast has been bred, but one and all diverge from the original, either in size, shape, or some other important particular.

GENUINE CHARACTERISTICS OF THE TRUE BEDLINGTON.

The model Bedlington should be rather long and small in the jaw, but withal muscular, the head high and narrow, crowned with the tuft of silky hair of lighter colour than the body, the eyes must be small, round, and rather sunk, and dull until excited, and then they are "piercers," the ears are filbert shaped, long, and hang close to the cheek, free of long hair, but slightly feathered at the tips; the neck is long, slender, but muscular, and the body well proportioned, slender and deep-chested; the toes must be well arched, legs straight, and rather long in proportion to the height, but not to any marked extent; the tail varies from 8 inches to 12 inches in length, is small and tapering, and free of feather. The best, and indeed only true, colours are—first, liver or sandy, and in either case the nose must be of a dark brown flesh colour, or secondly, a black blue, when the nose is black.

QUALITIES.

The Bedlington terrier is fast, and whether on land or water is equally at home. In appetite these dogs are dainty, and they seldom fatten, but experience has shown them to be wiry, enduring, and in courage equal to the bull dog. They will face almost anything, and I have known of a dog which would extinguish a lighted candle, or burning paper at his master's bidding. To their other good qualities may be added their marked intelligence and hostility to vermin of all forms and names. They will encounter the otter, fox, or badger, with the greatest determination.

OTHER BREEDS.

The linty haired, flaxen coloured terrier is common enough, but then he was never promoted, by good judges, to the dignity of a "Bedlington Terrier," except through courtesy. The breeding in and in alluded to is condemned as injurious beyond one strain.

PEDIGREE OF THE TRUE BEDLINGTONS.

The pedigree of Ainsley's Piper may be desirable as proving the facts contained in the above statements. Ainsley's Piper, by James Anderson's Piper, of Rothbury Forest, out of Ainsley's Phœbe, *alias* Coates's Phœbe; Anderson's Piper, by Ainsley's Peacham, out of Christopher Dixon's Phœbe, of Longhorsley; Peacham, by Cowen's Burdett, out of David Moffatt's bitch, of Howick; Dixon's Phœbe, by Sheawick's Matchem, of Longhorsley, out of John Dodd's Phœbe, of the same place; Matchem, by Edward Donkin's Pincher, of Flotterton, out of William Wardle's bitch, of Longframlington; Dodd's Phœbe, by Donkin's Old Peachem, out of Andrew Evan's Vixen, of Thropton; Vixen, by the miller's dog of Felton, out of Carr's bitch, of Felton Hall; Ainsley's Old Phœbe was by the Kennington dog, out of Andrew Riddle's Wasp, of Framlington; Wasp, by William Turnbull's Pincher, of Holystone, out of William Wardle's; Pincher, by Donkin's Old Peacham, out of Turnbull's Fan; Fan, by Myles's Matchem, of Netherwitton, by Squire Trevelyan's Flint: Donkin's Pincher, by Donkin's Old Peacham, continued from Ainsley's Crowner, by owner's Piper, out of owner's Meg;

Meg, out of Jin (own sister to Piper), by Robert Bell's Tugg, of Wingates; Tugg, by Robert Dixon's Dusty, of Longhorsley, out of a bitch of the Makepeace breed, presented by J. Ainsley to John Thompson.

OTTER-HUNTING IN THE LIDDEL AND THE ESK.

THE Carlisle otterhounds had a fine day's sport on the 12th of July, 1878. Meeting at Longtown, the drag was taken at Red Bank, and it was at first expected that a find would have been made in that favourite stronghold, but this expectation having been disappointed, a movement was made towards Canobie. Near the confluence of the Liddel and the Esk there was some lively dragging on the land, and all the way up to Hollows Bridge signs were abundant of more than one otter having been astir. It was not until the drain at Tarras Foot was reached that the otter was found. However, Rasper having entered the drain mouth was soon heard marking and baiting, and when he got out he bore numerous battle-scars upon his cheeks. The otter having been driven to the upper part of the drain excavations were made at different points. On trying the different sections with Smuggler and the terriers, it became evident that more than one otter was there, and the hounds were accordingly taken off to a distant part of the field. At length one was bolted from the high end of the drain, and was allowed to rush through the Tarras and get well on his way through the bushes and along the hill before the hounds were laid on. Then there was a fine burst amidst a scene of much excitement. The people by the Esk side had the satisfaction of seeing the otter come dashing down a steep bank and spring into the pool, with the whole pack following in full cry. After being hunted to and fro in the pool, the otter took down stream for a quarter of a mile and found shelter behind a rock, from which he was twice bolted by the terriers after a rather prolonged encounter. At length, finding the water too hot, he made across the pool, and took up a small rivulet that flows down a steep bank; thence he entered the wood above the highway, and went straight ahead for above half a mile at a pace that would have astonished those who still adhere to the popular delusion that an otter cannot run upon land. The tangled undergrowth of briers and ferns gave the otter some advantage over the hounds, as the latter could not get their noses down, but at length the fugitive came to a standstill and paused for breath. Then he made down a ravine towards the river, but, changing his mind, he turned back, and after another short run, was seized by the hounds and killed. The otter proved to be a female 15lbs weight, somewhat underfed, which perhaps accounts for her extraordinary activity and staying powers. There was a large crowd of spectators, and the excitement was intense, but perfect order was preserved, and everybody manifested the strongest desire that fairplay should be given to the otter, which, from first to last, was neither touched nor interfered with, except by the hounds and terriers. At the conclusion of the hunt, three cheers were given for the hounds, three for the master, and three for Sandy.

OTTER-HUNTING IN THE ALE WITH DR. GRANT'S OTTERHOUNDS.

The season was most brilliantly inaugurated in Ale water, when the gallant master of the hunt achieved a triumph on which he had long set his heart, long vowed he would some day accomplish, but which his friends who knew him best and admired him most ever declared could never be consummated even with all the daring and rare sporting qualifications which distinguish him, and the unexcelled metal, energy, perseverance, and pluck of his hounds and terriers. The drag was at first slow for a mile or two, but it improved as the pack went down the river, and had become so fast just before reaching Riddell that most of the followers on foot were thrown out, but the Doctor and his lad Walter being mounted kept close to the hounds. At length the spot, which proved to be the scene of action, was reached, at a part of the river where there is an overhanging bank for several yards, and the retreat seems so expressly intended for the otter that it can only be reached by a narrow hole at each end. Ringwood turned on his downward way and at once spoke out the cheerful sound, telling his delighted master that the game was near. The other dogs, excepting the bull dog Billy, were a good way in advance, probably because the varmint had first gone down and then doubled to his retreat. Ringwood made straight for the lower hole, which his huge bulk could not penetrate, as Billy was close after him, and filling up part of the space. Meanwhile the

Doctor stationed himself at the upper hole, and kept watch and ward up to his waist in water. To his great surprise the otter came out with Teddy the terrier hanging close under his throat, in which the little game one's dentals were grimly fixed. How and where Teddy got below the bank is one of the mysteries that will never be solved, but there he had certainly been to some purpose. The Doctor now saw the opportunity for which he had long waited, of catching a live otter, before him, and clutching the varmint by the neck, he ducked it and the terrier below the surface in hopes of obliging Teddy to quit his grip. Then a desperate struggle took place. Old Malakoff, Ruler, and Royal had just come back to the scene of the fray, and they furiously dashed at the Doctor's live prey, and, though Walter tried his best to keep them off, they resisted his utmost efforts, while master, hounds, and otter continued each struggling for the victory in the deep and rapid running stream. At last Walter got his coat off, and wrapped it round the otter under water, and the Doctor, keeping firm hold with his right hand on its throat, threw his left arm around it, and, clutching it to his breast, made for the land. Here Walter assisted the Doctor on his horse, but still the fierce hounds dashed round him open mouthed, determined to have their lawful prey, caring not for the whip which Walter plied most vigorously. At length the Doctor ordered a ruse to withdraw the attention of the pack, and sent Walter off tallyho-ing down the river. The ruse was successful, and the whole pack went off eager for another engagement. They must have found a second drag, for Walter could scarcely get a-head of them, and when he managed it at last, and brought them round, they were a long distance away. Left alone, when the excitement had subsided, the Doctor felt his left hand quite powerless, and discovered, for the first time, that it had been severely bitten. The varmint had also left its mark on his arm and breast, but the glorious excitement of the encounter had made him insensible to pain while the wounds were inflicted. The Doctor got home safely with his prize, a good deal exhausted by the engagement, but glorying in the long contemplated achievement of capturing an otter alive.

JOHN GALLON.

DEDICATED TO J. GRANT, ESQ., THE GALLANT MASTER OF THE TEVIOTDALE OTTER PACK.

JOHN GALLON, to whom the following song refers, was drowned in the river Lugar, South Ayrshire, Scotland, July 16th, 1873, while hunting the otter in company of Morton Macdonald Esq., of Largie Castle, and other famed sportsmen of North Britain.

For many years previous to his untimely death, he frequently hunted the Tyne, Reed, and other rivers of Northumberland.

Mr. Turnbull, the renowned otter hunter of North Tyne, for 27 years accompanied Gallon in nearly all his Border hunting excursions. He describes him as the Model Otter Hunter, a man of undaunted courage, and noble daring, a thorough gentleman in manner; of a kind disposition, and a veteran in the hunt. In short, Mr. Turnbull says, kind and good to the last. Frequently has he seen him when the otter was afoot and the hounds in full cry plunge into the deepest pools in pursuit of the sable game; scorning the use of the spear, he would tail the otter in the centre of the pack, and amidst the loud cheers of his followers bring the prize to land, and, in fair combat, try the courage of some favourite terrier.

Long will our Border huntsmen hold in remembrance the name of the gallant but unfortunate gentleman, who lies interred in Elsdon Churchyard, near Otterburn.

Some sing of bold Napoleon, that man of war-
    like name,
Of Wallace, Bruce, and Wellington, all heroes
    of great fame,
Ye otter-hunters one and all, in chorus join with
    me,
And we will of John Gallon sing, in numbers
    wild and free.

CHORUS.

Although John Gallon is no more, yet of him
    we will sing;
That gallant sportsman to the core, the otter-
    hunter King.

Northumbria's brave and dauntless son so gaily
    takes his way,
To hunt the Lugar's fatal stream at the first
    break of day.
With Starlight, Hopwood, Ringwood too, those
    hounds of glorious fame;
When Ormidale and Waterloo, the otter's drag
    proclaim.

Through shaggy cleugh, by willow stump, they hunt each hover true ;
Old Wellington and Mitford still the wily game pursue.
The music of each favourite hound the sleeping otter wakes,
He dives and tries his wildest shifts as his dark path he takes.

The sportsmen all join in the hunt, see where the bells they rise,
The otter's up and breathes, hurrah! the cheers they reach the skies ;
He's down again, and down the stream by rugged rock and scaur,
The gallant pack pursue their game in imag'ry of war.

Through darksome cleft, by thundering linn, are hounds and otter gone ;
John Gallon too so bold and true, to follow him not one.
But, O! in deep and treacherous pool, unseen to mortal eyes,
He's down, the daring hunter brave, he's down no more to rise.

No more we'll hear his cherry voice so early in the morn,

No more he'll wake the echoes wild, or wind his
    bugle horn,
No more the sportsmen of the North with Gallon
    will combine
To hunt the otter in the streams of Wansbeck,
    Reed, and Tyne.

THE CELEBRATED FOXHOUNDS OF EMMETHAUGH.

SPRUNG from a race of hounds which confer fame upon the packs of Slaley, Haydon, and Buccleugh; and shed a halo of hunting glory around the names of Forster, Dodd, Routledge, Hedley, Dagg, Robson, Jackson, Potts, Davison, and Scott, likewise around the name of their gallant owner William Robson, of Emmethaugh, best known on the Borders by the homely *soubriquet* of *Lang Will;* with whom and many others of the stalwart and wiry type of hunters, that hunt their hounds on foot, the author has had many a glorious foxhunt in the wilds of Kielder, North Tyne, Reed-water, and Liddesdale—the blood of this famous race of dogs has now asserted itself to be the hunting standard of the North, as they possess the scent, wind, pluck, speed, and endurance characteristic of the true Border Foxhound; and it may be interesting to the reader to learn that Tom Potts, of Burnmouth, the owner of "Towler"; and Yeddy Jackson, of Fairloans, (known by the cognomen of the *Hunter King*,) the owner of "Discord," were both hunting companions of James Davidson, of Hindlee, the undoubted prototype of Sir Walter Scott's Dandie Dinmont.

GENEALOGY OF THE HOUNDS.

MOUDY THE FIRST, by the Riggend (Tyne) dog, (a draft from the Haydon pack,) Gilbert Forster's "Winder," and out of the Hope House bitch, Walter Dodd's "Ruby." Ruby, by a south country dog, and out of the Crook bitch, William Routledge's "Lady." Lady, by the Bewshaugh dog, James Hedley's "Ruler."

MOUDY THE SECOND, by "Moudy the First," and out of the Yarrow Moor bitch, Matthew Dagg's "Ruby." Ruby, by the Riggend (Tyne) dog, (a draft from the Slaley pack,) Matthew Forster's "Ranter," and out of the Oakenshaw Burn bitch, Fergus Robson's "Ruby." Ruby, by the Burnmouth dog, Tom Potts' "Towler," and out of the Riggend (Kielder) bitch, John Robson's "Beeswing." Beeswing, by the Emmethaugh dog, William Robson's "Ragman," and out of the Fairloans bitch, Yeddy Jackson's "Discord." William Robson's Ragman, by the Riggend (Kieldar) dog, (a draft from the Buccleugh pack), John Robson's "Sealim," and out of the Riggend (Kielder) bitch, John Robson's "Ruby."

Moudy the Third, (winner of the Silver Cup at Gilsland, on the 22nd of October, 1868; beating a field of fourteen other hounds in a sixteen miles trail, over rough country, and covering the distance in fifty minutes,) by "Moudy the Second," and out of the Whookhope bitch, (a draft from the Haydon pack,) John Davison's "Ruby."

Moudy the Fourth, by "Moudy the Third," and out of the Oakenshaw Burn bitch, James Scott's "Rally."

Wyndham.

INSCRIBED TO JOSEPH ELLIOTT.

THIS celebrated trail hound (the subject of my song) belongs to Mr. John Armstrong of Scotscoltherd, near Haltwhistle, Northumberland. "Wyndham" was whelped on the 28th of July, 1873, sire "Seizer" of Redsyke, own brother to "Moudy III.," whose pedigree is given in this volume. (See the celebrated Foxhounds of Emmethaugh and their genealogy, page 100). Dam of Wyndham "Fateis," belonging to John Armstrong, of Scotscoltherd. Sire of "Fateis" Gilsland "Royal." Royal, by the Denton dog, Mr. Smith's "Towler," and out of the Rosehill bitch, Thomas Smith's "Charmer." "Towler," by the Samson Inn dog, Thomas Robson's "Towler," and out of "Doxy," belonging to John Bell. "Charmer" was by the Moscow dog, John Todd's "Dancer," and out of John Bell's

"Doxy." "Dancer" was by the Middleton dog "Spanker," and out of the Samson Inn bitch, Thomas Robson's "Ruby." Dam of "Fateis," Knarsdale "Ruby." "Wyndham" stands 24½ inches at the shoulder, is 28 inches round the body, and weighs 50lbs. It may be briefly stated, however, that the many victories achieved by "Wyndham" are, in a great measure, due to the care bestowed by the late Mr Henry Glenwright, and Mr Joseph Elliott, likewise Mr John Glenwright, in the training of the dog, who, for pluck, speed, and endurance has proved himself to be the best trail hound of his day, as the following records will show :—

Twice Brewed, 5th June, 1875, 15 dogs, 13 miles, Wyndham third,
Langholm, 27th July, 1875, 15 dogs, 8 miles, 17½ mins., Wyndham first.
Banks, 18th Sept., 1875, 9 dogs, 8 miles, 20 minutes, Wyndham first.
Slaggyford, 24th Sept., 1875, 15 dogs, 10 miles, 27 mins. Wyndham first.
Greenhead, 25th Sept., 1875, 13 dogs, 9 miles, 21 mins., Wyndham first.
Kielder, 1st Oct., 1875, 9 dogs, 16 miles, 41 minutes, Wyndham first.
Three Horse Shoes, South Tyne, 15th Oct., 1875, 9 dogs, 10 miles, 20 minutes, Wyndham first, Bewcastle dog second.

Tarset, 25th Feb., 1876, 14 miles, 34 minutes, Ruby first, Wyndham second.

Tarset, 10th March, 1876, 9 dogs, 17 miles, 49½ minutes, Smoker first, Wyndham second.

Stanners Burn, 11th March, 1876, 11 dogs, 10 miles, 21 minutes, Wyndham first, Ranger second.

King's Bridge Ford, 26th May, 1876, 8 dogs, 9 miles, 23 minutes, Wyndham first, Random second.

Armathwaite, 5th June, 1876, 10 dogs, 5 miles, 9 minutes, Wyndham first.

Armathwaite same day, 12 dogs, 6 miles, 14½ minutes, Wyndham first.

Troutbeck, 7th June, 1876, 13 dogs, 5 miles, 13 mins., Wyndham first.

Troutbeck, same day, 13 dogs, 5 miles, 14½ minutes, Wyndham first.

Langholm, 27th July, 1876, 20 dogs, 6 miles, 18 mins., Wyndham third.

Grasmere, 17th Aug., 1876, 20 dogs, 9 miles, 25 mins. Wyndham first, Crowner second, Barmaid third.

Slaggyford, 22nd Sept., 1876, 7 dogs, 10 miles, 28 mins. Wyndham first.

Greenhead, 23rd Sept., 1876, 7 dogs, 9 miles, 21 mins. Wyndham first.

Kielder, 6th Oct., 1876, 11 dogs, 18 miles, 61¼ minutes, Wyndham first, Irvine's Cleaver second, Mole's Famey third.

Gilsland, 13th Oct., 1876, 13 dogs, 12 miles, 35 minutes, Wyndham first.

Three Horse Shoes, South Tyne, 17th Nov., 1876, 5 dogs, 10 miles, 27½ minutes, Wyndham first.

Alwinton, 27th March, 1877, 14 dogs, 9 miles, 25 mins., Wyndham first, Tinker second. Several of the dogs were thrown off this trail in consequence of coming across the drag of a fox.

Alston, 2nd April, 1877, 8 dogs, 8 miles, 26 minutes, Wyndham third.

King's Bridge Ford, 5th April, 1877, 8 dogs, 10 miles, 30 minutes, Music first, Wyndham third.

Waterhouse, 14th April, 1877, 14 dogs, 9 miles, 27 minutes, Wyndham first.

Burgh Marsh, 30th April, 1877, 13 dogs, 8 miles, 20 minutes, Wyndham first,

On the last-named day, the accession of St. George Henry, Earl of Lonsdale, to the title and privileges of Lord of the Barony of Burgh, was celebrated by sports on Burgh Marsh in accordance with the ancient custom. From north and south, from east and west, excursionists in thousands flocked to the scene of amusement. The Earl of Lonsdale, with a brilliant party, including the Duke of Montrose, the Earl and Countess of Bective, Lord Muncaster, Lord and Lady Hill, the Hon. W. Lowther, M.P., Miss Lowther, the Hon. H. Lowther, and Mrs. Cavendish Bentinck, went down by the road, decked with yellow roses, which Messrs. E. F. Fairbairn and Son's had had the honour of presenting in the morning. The course was kept by the county police, aided by Lord Lonsdale's huntsman, and a couple of his "whips," who, dressed in scarlet coats, mounted on splendid hunters, and armed with hunting whips, rendered valuable assistance in keeping the crowd back, and, on the victory of Wyndham, the excitement was intense, and here, as at Grasmere, Mr. Elliott and the dog were surrounded by lords and ladies, artists, and the general crowd, all eager to get a glimpse of the winner, and it was counted an honour even to touch the gallant hound.

Troutbeck, 23rd May, 1877, 8 dogs, 5 miles, 12 mins. Wyndham first.

Troutbeck, same day, 7 dogs, 4 miles, 12 minutes, Wyndham first.

Twice-Brewed, 16th June, 1877, 8 miles, 24½ minutes, Wyndham first.

Gothland, 29th June, 1877, 6 miles straight out, 14 minutes, Wyndham won by 4 minutes, Center second.

From Paddaburn to Kirkcambeck, 19th July, 1877, 10 miles, 25 minutes, Routledge's Ranter first, his Random second, Wyndham third.

Langholm, 27th July, 1877, 14 dogs, 7 miles, 17 minutes, Wyndham first.

Red Dial, 1st August, 1877, 5 dogs, 6 miles, 16 minutes, Wyndham first.

Talkin Tarn, 6th August, 1877, 13 dogs, 9 miles, 26 mins., Routledge's Ranter first, Wyndham second,

Talkin Tarn, same day, 13 dogs, 5 miles, 14 minutes, Routledge's Random first, Wyndham second.

Grasmere, 23rd August, 1877, 9 miles, 40 minutes, Crowner first, Wyndham second.

Langholm, 1st Sept., 1877, 12 dogs, 4 miles, 16 minutes, Cleaver first, Wyndham fourth.

Slaggyford, 21st Sept., 1877, 10 dogs, 12 miles, 34 mins. Wyndham won by 5 minutes, 39 seconds.

Stanners Burn, 29th Sept., 1877, 12 miles, 35 minutes, Wyndham won by 4 minutes.

Rosehill, 5th October, 1877, 10 miles, 35 minutes, Wyndham first.

Newcastleton, 13th October, 1877, 12 dogs, 12 miles, Wyndham first, Cleaver second.

Common House, 20th October, 1877, Challenge Medal. Conditions: The winner of the Challenge Medal will be subject to accepting a challenge from any other person for not less than £10, and within nine days' notice, for the ensuing twelve months. Security must also be given for the refunding of the Medal in case of being beaten within the twelve months. Nine dogs ran, distance 10 miles, time 32 minutes, Wyndham first, Damsel second. No challenge.

Shop Ford, 16th Nov., 1877, 7 dogs, 10 miles, 31 mins., Wyndham first, Young Tinker second.

Shop Ford, same day, 6 dogs, 5 miles, 15½ minutes, Wyndham first.

Moorcock, 15th Feb., 1878, 7 dogs, 9 miles, 29 minutes, Wyndham first.

King's Bridge Ford, 22nd March, 1878, 9 miles, 29 mins., Gelderd's Ranter first, Wyndham third.

Tarset, 23rd March, 1878, 7 dogs, 16 miles, 60 minutes, Wyndham third.

Stanners Burn, 29th March, 1878, 7 dogs, 10 miles, 29 minutes, Wyndham first.

Lyne Bank, 5th April, 1878, 14 dogs, 10 miles, 28 mins., Wyndham first.

Bellingham, 8th May, 1878, 8 dogs, 12 miles, 35 minutes, Wyndham first.

Armathwaite, 10th June, 1878, 7 dogs, 4 miles, 13 mins., Wyndham first.

Armathwaite, same day, 7 dogs, 4½ miles, 13½ minutes, Wyndham first.

Troutbeck, 12th June, 1878, 7 dogs, 4½ miles, 14 mins., Wyndham first.

Troutbeck, same day, 7 dogs, 4½ miles, 14 minutes, Wyndham first.

Langholm, 27th July, 1878, 16 dogs, 7 miles, 20 minutes, Cleaver first, Wyndham fifth.

Newcastleton, 9th August, 1878, 11 dogs, 12 miles, 40 minutes, Young Tinker first, Wyndham second.

Common House, 31st August, 1878, 9 dogs, 12 miles, 48 minutes, Young Tinker first, Wyndham second.

Common House, same day, 8 dogs, 4 miles, 15 minutes, Wyndham first.

Irthing Vale Hunt Meeting, 2nd May, 1879, Mr. Armstrong's Wyndham first, 18 dogs ran.

Abbey Bridge End, Lanercost, 23rd May, 1879, 8 dogs, Wyndham first, Ranter second. Won by a mile.

Royal Hotel, June 2nd, 1879, 4 dogs, 5 miles, 15 mins., Wyndham first.

Penruddock, 2nd June, 2 dogs, 4 miles, 12½ minutes. Wyndham first.

Troutbeck, June 4, 1879, 6 dogs, 5 miles, 14¼ minutes, Wyndham first, Music of Carlisle second, 15 mins.

Troutbeck, same day, 5 dogs, 5 miles, 14½ minutes, Wyndham first, Music of Carlisle second, 16 mins.
Kirby Stephen, 5th June, 1879, 4 dogs, 9 miles, 33 mins., Wyndham first, Rattler (out of Barmaid) second, 40 minutes.
Melkridge, 20th Sept., 1879, 8 miles, 7 dogs, 23 mins., Wyndham won by 2½ minutes.
Slaggyford, 26th Sept., 1879, 10 miles, 7 dogs, 27½ mins., Wyndham won by 200 yards.

CUPS.

Below is a list of the Cups won by Wyndham, bearing the following inscriptions :—

Langham Hound Race, 1875, John Armstrong's Wyndham.
Kielder Hound Race, 1875, John Armstrong's Wyndham.
South Tyne Hound Race, 1876, John Armstrong's Wyndham.
Greenhead Hound Race, 1876, John Armstrong's Wyndham.
Kielder Hound Race, 1876, John Armstrong's Wyndham.
Presented by Mr. William Sharp, of Park House, to the South Tyne Hound Race, 1876, John Armstrong's Wyndham.
Twice Brewed Hound Race, 1877, |John Armstrong's Wyndham.

Langham Hound Race, 1877, John Armstrong's Wyndham.

Red Dial Hound Race, 1877, John Armstrong's Wyndham.

Newcastleton Hound Race, 1877, John Armstrong's Wyndham.

Shop Ford Hound Race, 1877, John Armstrong's Wyndham.

Lyne Bank Hound Race, 1878, John Armstrong's Wyndham.

Royal Hotel, Matterdale, 1879, John Armstrong's Wyndham.

Ye gallant sportsmen one and all, whoever that you be,
That love a foxhunt and a trail, in chorus join with me,
And we will of a trail dog sing, a hound of glorious fame,
John Armstrong is his owner and Wyndham is his name.

CHORUS.

Success to bonnie Wyndham, that fleet and gallant hound;
He's won his weight in cups and gold, and is with glory crowned.
At Langholm and Newcastleton, he prov'd his speed so true;

At Stanners Burn and Alwinton, South Tyne
and Kielder too;
At Gilsland, and at Shopford, and Slaggyford
likewise;
At Troutbeck, and at Kingbrig Ford, he bore
away the prize.

Then again at Grasmere, the hounds are now in
sight,
And bounding hearts in gallant breasts expand-
ing with delight,
The cheers of thousands rent the air upon that
glorious day,
When bonnie Wyndham beat the field, and took
the prize away.

Then look at him at Burgh Marsh, when all the
hounds of fame,
To try their speed with Wyndham, from far
and near they came;
The gallant hound outstrips them all, as o'er the
sward he flies;
Hurrah! hurrah! he wins again, the cheers they
reach the skies.

Little "Fateis" was his dam, and "Seizer" was
his sire,

From them he got his wind and speed, from them
    he got his fire,
For all the cups that he has won, and prizes too
    in gold,
On the hunting scroll of fame his name it is en-
    roll'd.

Then here's to every trail dog that has with
    Wyndham run,
Their owners and their trainers, here's to them
    every one;
And likewise to our Border sports, I hope they'll
    never fail,
Long life to every one that likes a foxhunt and a
    trail.

The Kielder Hunt.

DEDICATED TO JOHN ROBSON.

Hark! hark! I hear Lang Will's clear voice
    sound through the Kielder glen,
Where the raven flaps her glossy wing and the
    fell fox has his den;

There the shepherds they are gathering up wi'
    monie a guid yauld grew,
An' wiry terrier game an' keen, an' fox-hund
    fleet and true.

CHORUS.

    Hark away! hark away!
    O'er the Bonnie Hills o' Kielder, hark away.

There's Moudy frae Emmethaugh an' Royal frae
    Bakethinn,
There's hunds frae Reed an' Kielderhead, an'
    Ruby by the Linn;
An' hunds of fame frae Irthingside, they try baith
    moss an' crag,
Hark! hark! that's Moudy's loud clear note, he
    has bold Reynard's drag.

Away an' away o'er hill and dale, an' up by
    yonder stell,
The music o' the gallant pack resounds o'er
    muir an' dell;
See yon herd callant waves his plaid, list yon
    loud tally-ho,
The fox is up an' breaks away o'er the edge o'
    Hawkhope Flowe.

Hark forrit, hark! ye gallant hunds, hark on-
   wart, hark away,
He kens the hauds on Tosson hills, he kens the
   holes at Rae;
There's no a den roun' the Kailstane but he
   kens weel I trow,
An' a' the holes on Lariston he kens them thro'
   and thro'.

There's Wannys Crags, an' Sewingshields, and
   Christenbury too,
Or if he win to Hareshaw Linn ye may bid him
   adieu;
The Key-Heugh an' the Cloven-Crags, the Cove,
   an' Darnaha',
Chatlehope-Spout an' the Wily-holes, auld foxy
   kens them a'.

Away an' away o'er bank an' brae they drive the
   wily game,
Where Moudy, Ruby, Royal still uphaud their
   glorious fame;
An' see the lish yald shepherd lads how Monk-
   side heights they climb,
They're the pride o' a' the borders wide for wind
   and wiry limb.

Thro' yon wild glen they view him now right for
   the Yearning Linn,

By cairn an' crag, o'er moss and hagg, sae
    glorious is the din ;
Weel dune, hurrah! they've run him doun, yon's
    Moudy twirls him now,
The hunt is dune, his brush is wun, I hear the
    death hal-loo.

Here's to Will o' Emmelhaugh, he is a sports-
    man true,
Here's to Robie o' Bakethinn, an' Rob o' Kielder,
    too ;
At the Hope, Bewshaugh, an' Kersie Cleuch,
    Skaup, Riggend, an' the Law,
In Tyne, an' Reed, and Irthinghead, they're
    gallant sportsmen a'.

LETTERS TO THE AUTHOR.

                      Hawick, Saturday Night.

DEAR MR. ARMSTRONG,—I have carefully compared your *proof* with my Records, and also with "Stonehenge," and find the genealogy of the Dandie Dinmonts *strictly correct*.

I turned up some old reprints by accident the other day, of which there are a few on Otterhunting.

It appears that my heart disease had been gaining ground, and my health falling off from it, as far back as 1863, so it is no wonder I am now so completely winged.—Ever yours truly,

JOHN GRANT.

THE DANDIE DINMONTS.

Copy of Letter from Lieut. Colonel Cust to the Author, Jan. 31, 1879.

Harewood Bridge, Harewood, Leeds.

MR. ARMSTRONG,—I have been a long time returning you all the letters and papers you sent me about the "Dandie Dinmont Terriers," but I assure you I have read them with the greatest interest. I have taken the liberty of copying out your points of a Dandie. I hope you will not object my having done so, but if you do I will destroy it. I think you should send to "The Field" the points of the Dandie Terrier, for really the nonsense that has been written about them is past everything. I recollect some years ago, Mr Nicholl Milne, of Faldonside, having what he called pure Dandies, and Mr James Kerss, gamekeeper, of Bowhill, also, but they were not the least like your puppy, or like one another. Your puppy (or rather my puppy now), has a good blue-grey coat, black claws, good dark hazel coloured eyes as bright as diamonds, with good strong legs, and a long, low, strong body; he is growing as level as possible, and is a famous little fellow. Mr Milne's dogs were more fawn than mustard, on a longer leg, with a shorter back than your breed, and rather a less broken coat. Mr Kerss's, on the contrary, were of a light fawn colour, with very silky coats and nasty short jaws, with round heads like frogs, very hard and very quarrelsome, and yet not capable from the nature of the coat to stand real cold. The hair was more like a soft flaxen wig. I have had many a hunt both on the English and Scotch Border hills after the foxes with the hounds at Langholm, Old Kyle of Broadlee; Ballantine, of Shaws; Robson, of Kielder, and his brother of Lowshield Green. Old Kyle's favourite hound Ringwood always slept in his bed. I fear much of this good old Border sport has not gone on of late years as it used to do formerly, for some reason or other. From the photograph you sent me of Dr. Grant, I think he must have been the son of my old friend Dr. Grant, a fine hale sportsman of sixty or so. Twenty years ago he used to hunt with the Duke of Buccleuch's hounds, and was famed for his terriers. You had better let me know when you have another litter of Dandies to dispose of.—Yours truly,

J. FRANCIS CUST.

MR. ARMSTRONG.

COPY OF AUTOGRAPH LETTER FROM THE COUNTESS OF DARWENTWATER TO THE AUTHOR.

The Countess of Darwentwater thanks Mr Armstrong for his poetical lines, and furthermore will remember with grateful recollection the homage he offers to the memory of her chivalrous great grandfather, James, Third Earl of Darwentwater, who died a martyr for his country, his king, and the truth, on the 24th of

February, 1716. Mr Armstrong's verses awaken feelings of emotion in the Countess—who could wish the following could be written in gold on the royal door at Windsor Castle, to *remind* Kings and Queens that *mercy* and *justice* is their mission here on earth.

<blockquote>
Is it a King the woful widow hears?
Is it a King drys up the orphan's tears?
Is it a King regards the clyents cry,
Gives life to him by law condemn'd to die?
</blockquote>

I send an abridged pedigree, which is better than the one you have from the newspaper slip. I beg of you to read the Hon. William Radcliffe's last will—the original covers nine sheets of parchment written in a fine style of christian language. He was one of the trustees for my grandfather. The sheet which covered the Earl is a sad relic to look upon, which I am in possession of.

A. C. of D——.

Temperance Hotel, Innerleithen,
Dec. 13th, 1877.

DEAR MR. ARMSTRONG,—I am sometimes wondering if your Border harp is now unstrung, as I have seen nothing from your truly poetic pen since the publication of "Wanny Blossoms." I have enjoyed the reading of these "Blossoms" over and over again. Therefore, I hope that you are still on the Mount of Parnassus, and that you will continue to sing of your native Borderland. Does your muse never think of winging across the Border line into the land of the Armstrongs, the land of your sires, or has your branch of the clan been so long on the southern side as to induce you to forego all connection with our Scottish side. May I ask what has become of your true heroine "Lizzie Storey," she who you have so tenderly and becomingly embalmed in song. I may tell you that I have long been considerably interested in the exploits and haunts of the Old Border Smugglers. Now I see that in your volume you mention the "Whisky Syke." Could you kindly favour me with the traditions (if any) about the "Syke;" how it got the name, and where it is. Excuse me for troubling you, but believe me to be, yours truly,

ROBERT MURRAY.

GALLANT RUN WITH THE NORTH TYNE AND IRTHINGHEAD HOUNDS.

[THE following description of a foxhunt and a day with the hounds were contributed to the papers sometime ago by the writer; and at the request of my hunting friends, I give them both as a reprint.]

"DEATH OF "BURNT TOM."

Arouse, "Burnt Tom," my game old fox, the last time from thy den,
For Lang Will's voice is sounding far through Leasburn's shaggy glen,
He's cheering on the gallant hounds, I hear fleet Moudy's cry,
Take thy last look of cairn and brook, ere sunset thou shalt die.

The hounds were uncoupled at Cranecleugh, on Tuesday morning, when they soon found a drag, hunting it slowly over the heights to Leasburn, but it is too old and cold. Let us lift them, and try down by the Forks, where the holes are barred. Presently they give tongue that makes music fit to lift your cap, and tells that the scent is new and warm. Away they go, streaming over the knowes, heads up; that's him, Ringwood lad. Hark! together, hark! Tallyho! he's away, and, by Jove, it's "Burnt Tom," the very fox that beat the dogs so often last year. Yonder he goes, with the beauties at his kenspecklt brush, through the deer park, and past Mouncies. They will kill him; not yet, he's on past Otterstone Lea,

Away, away, o'er bank and brae, they drive the wily game.
Where Moudy, Ruby, Royal, still uphold their glorious fame.

He means either Whickhope Linn, or the holes above Emmethaugh. He takes the east; they are nearest. Well done, Tom, but are you safe? Wait awhile, here comes Jock o' the Houp, with Venom, and in she goes, and comes out sorely dragglt. She cannot find him, shakes herself, and in again. There is a noise in the hole, the terrier has found him. Now, silence, and he'll maybe leap; there he's out. Ruby and Royal make a dash at him, but he clears them among the scroggs, and boldly faces the steep brae, and on to the open bent with all the hounds after him. Isn't yon glorious! Yonder they go, back past Otterstone Lea and Mouncies again. See yon lad of Yarrow, he's going like the wind, leaving Matt of Otterstone Lea, Tom Breckney, and Wannie, but Matt is sair hoppled; he has a grew in a string, and the clogs on, but take time, he will get the galloway if he was at the house; but, ah! waes me, his sister has been out for a morning scamper, her faither has met her, and he's on to the beast, and away after the "hunds." "The deil tak' me faither, he'll kill the galloway. He's sixteen stane onyway, forebye the heavy side saddle." The gallant little pack are still crushing on their fox, aiming now for Kersenberrie, or maybe Lisha holes, or Witch Linn. But they are too far, so he changes his course, and tries the holes at the Forks. Ha! my old boy, there is a sneck before thy snout. Away down the glen, his relentless pursuers hot on him, past Ferny Knowe, and into Looie wood, where they rattle him round for a while, then all is silent. Is it a kill, or is he lost? Try the scroggs, rough heather, and all the likely ling. Sweep the hounds round the outside of the wood. Silent still; lost he must be, but how or where? Try again, it is useless wishing better luck next time. There is nothing but home for us. The guidwife of Looie is coming out of the byre, when Lang Will shouts " my woman, hae ye seen aucht o' the fox?" "Fox, aye, losh, man he's in the byre here, lying afore the cow; but o' man, Will, dinna kill the puir beastie." But Will was soon into the byre and out again with the beastie in his brawny hand, soothing the feelings of the good woman with the assurance that the fox should have a fair chance for his life. "Now, get hauld o' the huns," while Will slips him quietly over the dyke into the haugh. But the dogs wind their game once more, and are bad to hold. They let them away. See they are on him again, full cry, through the wood and past Ferny Knowe again; over the hill, down to the burn, and along the edge of the shingles. Go into him now, my dogs of war. The blood of old Moudy for ever. Over the burn, and on to the top of the scaur. Over he goes, hounds and all, where they ran into as fine a specimen of the greyhound fox as ever footed the heather. The "steekers" in are now up, let us see who we have. Here is Jock o' the Houp, Matt o' Otterstone Lea, and Jimmie Sisterson of Yarrow, three wiry-looking lads, fleet as deer, and winded as Arabs; Adam of Smail, Tom Armstrong, Wannie, Tom Lowrie, Lang Will, W. Little, and Mitt of Cranecleugh, his homespun grey belted with a pair of couples over a back like a barn board, and a breast like a Kyloe bullock. With hearty acclamation the skin of the devoted fox is awarded to Wannie, who sends it away to be preserved, and the many grand hunts with "Burnt Tom," and the last run for his life, will long be remembered in North Tyne.

The Morning Drag.

Air: "Whittle Scroggs."

Come away with me my boys, once for hunting joys,
   The hounds o'er the bent they are bounding.
Away by yonder crag, they are on the morning drag,
   So sweetly their music is sounding.

Then listen to each hound as they try the rimey ground,
   Hark! to Moudy's loud note in the number;
It's Lang Will's voice we hear, the gallant pack to cheer,
   That will waken the fox from his slumber.

That's Seizer calls him now, Ringwood and
    Royal too,
And Ruby's clear note is proclaiming
That the drag is new and warm, our bounding
    hearts to charm,
For the wild Christenbury now aiming.

Through the scroggy glen, how they hunt him
    to his den,
Shall be told both in song and in story,
And when the fox shall die, our shouts will
    reach the sky,
Then each sportsman will be in his glory.

A DAY WITH THE NORTH TYNE AND IRTHINGHEAD FOXHOUNDS.

AT the Whisky Syke the hounds were lows'd by Walter Dodd, the gallant huntsman of the pack, where, spreading away to the hill of Burnt Tom, they hit off a cold drag, hunting it slowly but surely past Yet Burn Spout and Upper Longhouse. At this time we hear tallyho in the direction of

Christenbury Crags, where a fox had been seen stealing away, but the hounds, true to their own instinct, keep on the old drag up the Long Rigg, and across Lewisburn, winding away up Merlin's Cleugh, where the notes of the beasties waken bold Reynard from his slumbers, and they view him away. leaving Glendue to the left, the music of the gallant pack ringing far and wide, bringing the footmen "frae a' the airts the win' can blaw," some from the heights above Bewcastle, and some from the heathery crests overlooking Liddesdale. Fox and dogs are now on the Oakenshaw side of the hill, over bent and broken braes, up the burn at a killing pace, on to the heights and past Elliot's Pikes, where "my nabs" ran to ground. What is to be done? Must we try if he will bolt? Yes; here is "Tommy" the Bewshaugh terrier, that reminds us of an otter with his long body and short legs, a real Dandie Dinmont all over; he is in, and quickly challenges the game, but Tommy is too big and cannot get up to the mark. It is perhaps as well for the fox, as there is danger in those fiery eyes and cruel-looking jaws. Try Wasp, of Tarnbecks. She is at him, but comes out again, apparently not liking the job, but in a short time returns to the attack, and closes with him this time. Call back the hounds, and keep quiet; yonder he is out. "Young Moudy," a pup of eight months, is laid on, and is tearing away and giving mouth grandly, reminding us of the glorious days of his illustrious sire, old "Moudy," of Emmethaugh, and equally celebrated "Scizer" † of Redsyke. The rest of the dogs are now laid on, and are down to the burn in full cry, when a trial of speed among the shepherd lads takes place in anticipation of the brush. The chase is fast and furious, and the fox, finding his pursuers too near him, turns up the syke and takes refuge in some rocks near the Willow Bog. The terrier brigade are again brought up, and lay siege to the enemy, but it is useless. Cut he will not come, and appears to have made up his mind to die rather than again try his speed before the remorseless foe awaiting him outside, eager for his blood. "Howking" tools are brought from the house, likewise a good supply of "starkning" and mountain dew. Work now commences in earnest; Wasp marks him, and an opening is made to the spot, but he shifts. The terrier is at him again, and comes out with a slight scratch on the nose. Redsyke, with a sly smile, remarks, "Marcy, Jimmie, hoo she's punish'd!" The slit of the crag is now opened, Rock, the Redsyke terrier, is now put in, and, as if to revenge past defeats and insults, at once goes into his fox, when

† "Seizer," sire of Wyndham, the renowned trail hound.

a real battle royal takes place, and they are at a dead lock. Tarnbecks creeps in, tails the terrier, and draws the combatants to the light of day. The hounds are again collared, and the fox carried down the brae. Now he is off, hounds, hunters, collies, terriers, all in full chorus and hot pursuit, in true imagery of war. Royal of Tarnbecks is leading. Well done—the Scotscoltherd dog passes him. Now Ruby of The Hope is past them both; Tarnbeck Scott is running like a redskin, as if he would outstrip both the hounds and the Oakenshaw lad that set away the fox; wild are the shouts and glorious is the din. "Hurrah!" there is the death hallo—it is over—and Watt of Oakenshaw Burn takes the coveted fur.

The Tarsettearian Fox.

INSCRIBED TO THOMAS ARMSTRONG, THE CELEBRATED
FOXHUNTER OF NORTH TYNE.

The various incidents described in the following song occurred at the famous foxhunt held at Earls Seat, 20th March, 1875. The brilliant run was witnessed by the writer, who also was in the midst of the fun at the finish.

THE Tarset men a hunting went,
   Sae early in the morn,
Wi' Ruby, Royal, Windham, too,
   Away by Hunter Burn.
The joyfu' soond of horn an' hund,
   Rous'd reynard frae the rocks,
At break o' day they view'd away
   A Tarsettearian Fox.

Over hills, thro' dusky dells,
   By monie a cairn and scaur,
The little pack pursue their game,
   Like gallant dogs of war,
Till on the Belling's shaggy brow
   Some o' the glaiky brocks
Did scrauch an' shoot, an' scar aboot,
   That Tarsettearian Fox.

Away o'er bent an' heathery heights,
    The dogs and fox are gane;
Till little Ruby o' the Kame
    Was huntin' him alane.
When in the shire of Donkleywood,
    The Tyne lads cam in flocks;
Horse, fut, an' hun' join'd in the run
    Of that Tarsettearian Fox.

Reynard noo ance mair heads back
    Straight for his hielan' sheil;
Frae mouie a scrauch an' fearfu' yell,
    Eneuch to flay the deil.
He leaves them a', far, far awa',
    Hunds, Sandys, Wulls, and Jocks,
O! joy of joys, he's hol'd, my boys,
    That Tarsettearian Fox.

The hunds an' hunters then cam up,
    The howkin it began;
Some swore the fox should hae fair-play,
    Some wanted a neck hunn.
Then Andra Robson rampit oot,
    Sic thunnerin stanes in blocks;
He ript the haggs and splet the crags,
    For that Tarsettearian Fox.

Stand back! stand back! then some did shoot,
    When the terriers were set in;

The gallant fox was bagg'd at last,
    The fun it did begin.
The Tyne lads and the Tarset men
    They neckit like game cocks,
" Kame Wully" stud stagnatit *see*
    Ower that Tarsettearian Fox.

Tom Armstrong grippit still his game,
    Ye never saw sic fun,
That Yarrow cheil, Jim Sisterson,
    Spanghew'd a Tarset hun'.
The Meun gript Moffat by the neck,
    An' swore he'd clean their clocks,
Some gat the skin peel'd off their shin
    Ower that Tarsettearian Fox.

Peace was then proclaim'd ance mair,
    The fox was set away;
Horse, fut, an' hunds, a' after him,
    In wild and grand array.
But frae the rush he sav'd his brush,
    And hol'd in yonder rocks;
Au' hid his nose frae frien's and foes,
    That Tarsettearian Fox.

The Trial of Wee Piper.

The subject of the following song is a Terrier dog that was banished, by order of the Gamekeeper, from Kielderhead, on account of its supposed poaching propensities. The poor animal subsequently found a home at the Shaws in Liddesdale.

Wee Piper he wander'd awa,
   And far up Whyte Kielder did daunder,
He nozzl't a rabbit or twa,
   For the sake o' the fun an' the plunder.

Black Sandy seun heard o' the raid,
   An' swore he wad hang the wee huel;
A gallows sae hie then he made,
   To fulfil his fell purpose sae cruel.

That Piper had trespass'd sae far,
   Of that there could be no denial;
The herds then stud up for the Tarr,
   And threep'd he should hae a fair trial.

Then Piper was put in the box,
   Wi' his tail round his claws like a cat;
Still hoping the frasy might turn out a hoax,
   Wi' patience puir fallow he sat.

If Lucas had been on the bench,
  Some slight hopes o' mercy might been;
But the case must be tried by the law that is
    Lynch,
  Where mercy is not to be seen.

Then guilty or not, the question was put,
  But the prisoner said not a word;
The jury then saw that his conscience was cut,
  When they cried oot, he's guilty my Lord.

The evidence then was summed up,
  An' justice well'd up to the brim;
When Sandy gat up an' put on the black cap,
  To pronounce the dread sentence on him.

Will o' West Kielder sat pale as the moon,
  In suspense he did keep in his breath;
Musing the while if nought could be done
  To ward off the fell sentence of death.

Then Mitt o' Skaup sae bauldly stood up,
  An' spak oot sae free an' sae ready,
That he'd kend wee Piper sin he was a pup,
  An' aye thought him sae harmless *it did he.*

Then Sandy he paused an' to Piper said,
  Your death will be no gain to me;
And by what Mitt has said, your life will be sav'd,
  But you shall be sent o'er the sea.

The case it is proven, the verdict is given,
   That you've been the cause o' this strife,
And to-morrow at sunrise, you off shall be driven,
   For the term of your natural life.

Wee Piper's Letter.

Noo, Wully, my man, when this comes to han',
   Ye'll be thinkin' I'm ower the wotter,
But I gae them the slip an' lap oot o' the ship,
   And swam to the land like an otter.
An' I've trampit thro' touns whair ill-deedy louns
   Shoutit Peachim, an' Pincher, an' Viper,
An' man, Wull, sic dougs wi' short cuttit lugs—
   I thocht they wad eaten Wee Piper.

I waddl't away by nicht an' by day,
   O'er crags, thro' moss-haggs, an' lang heather,
Till I wan to the Shaws, gae thin i' the jaws,
   An' the skin aff my feet a' thegither;
Sae couthiely then they cried on me ben—
   An' a cheil bein' here frae the Kinmont,
Wha kens a' my kin frae the Knott to Bakethinn,
   An' he threeps I'm a real Dandie Dinmont.

Here's milk an' here's meal, an' braxie as weel,
  And the Laird is a gallant foxhunter;
Here's horses an' hun's an' cudgels an' guns,
  Sae I'm safe frae Black Sandy this wunter.
I heard the Laird swear, if Sandy comes here,
  He shall rue that he ever left Riddle,
For he'll lowse every hun', and he'll bet fifty pun',
  That he never mair crosses the Liddel.

An' Willie, my man, I've fixt on a plan,
  And I'll tell ye my mind in a blinkin',
I ken o' a ploy that'll suit ye, my boy,
  An' monie mair tae, I'm thinkin'.
We'll raise a' the hun's an' ilk tyke that runs,
  An' a' the yauld hunters, my mannie,
Rouse Liddel an' Reed, an' a' the Tyne-head,
  An' we'll hae a graun' huntin' wi' Sawnie.

Rouse a' swoft o' fit—bring Jock, Gead, an' Mitt,
  An' Bowman, an' Ned, an' the Pether;
To the fun an' the din the Daggs 'll a' rin'
  Like bucks spankin' ower the heather.
Seek the Skinner an' Jim, an' Larry, bring him,
  "Let the day be a regular fielder;"*
Seek Wull-o'-the-Raw, an' Wannie an' a',
  An' we'll hunt Sandy oot o' the Kielder.

  * Quotation from Mr Milburn.

POSTSCRIPT.

Seek Yed o' Ravenshill, an' Rob an' Lang Will,
    Auld Jowhn o' the Houp, an' Lang Sally,†
An' Rob o' Bakethinn—I ken he'll steek in,
    To gie the Black Loon a guid rally.
Bring ilka guid Tarr an' a' dougs o' war,
    An' Clapperton tae, an' auld Tartar;
At first peep o' day we'll set Sandy away,
    And hunt him richt ower the Cairter.

The Fishin', My Lad.

By the clear winding streamlet the daisy now
    springs,
On the soft mossy brae-side the sweet primrose
    hings;
Wi' the cowslip an' gowan the green-sward is
    clad,
Sae we'll away off to the fishin', my lad,

CHORUS.

The fishin', my lad, the fishin', my lad,
We'll away off to the fishin', my lad.
We'll gan to the streams where there's fun to be
    had,
Then come on wi' me to the fishin' my lad.

† William Dodd, of Cairnsyke, the famous foxhunter.

Wi' the bonnie red-hackle an' dotterel sae fine,
An' black speyder too, lad, we'll tackle wer line.
The lavrock is singin' sae joyfu' and glad,
Then come on wi' me to the fishin', my lad.

In the Reed an' the Wansbeck, the bonnie troot
    thrives;
In yon lang peuls an' streams, where the dun
    otter dives,
It's there, where the big yellow-fin bends the
    gad,
Then come on wi' me to the fishin', my lad.

In the Jed, an' the Liddel, and Coquet sae clear,
North Tyne an' Whyte Kielder, there's troots
    never fear.
We'll gan to the streams where there's fun to be
    had,
Then come on wi' me to the fishin', my lad.

The Wonderful Book and Wily Wully's Confession.

"Sound the trumpet, beat the drum,"
The Wonderful Book at last is come;
Toot, toot thy horn, oh, glorious fame!
Frae pole to pole my praise proclaim.

Frae north to south, from east to west,
O'er every hill and mountain's crest;
It's the queerest book, sirs, ever ye saw,
By Curly Jock and Wull o' the Raw.

But I'll confess and tell ye plain,
Half o' the verses are no my ain;
Frae Burns I've stown monie a line,
An' Tannahill too, an' ca'd them mine.
And weav'd them deftly thro' an' thro',
Wi' sanctified warps an' wifts o' blue;
Sae then buck-up baith ane an a',
For Curly Jock and Wull o' the Raw.

The queerest trick, sirs, ever I play'd,
Since I began the rhymin' trade;
When frae Drumlee I stole, ye ken,
Wee Piper's farewell to Kielder Glen.
Od! Wull says I, at last incog,
That's ower guid for onie dog;
To the shepherd's farewell I weav'd it braw,
An' then cried weal deun Wull o' the Raw.

To the *Herald* then the lines I sent,
Sae sleek an slee for them to prent;
But ah! waes me, that prenter's deil,
And Dandie Dinmont awfu' cheil,

In next week's sheet they plain tauld me
I'd stown some verses frae Drumlee,
Eha ! I seyght when the trickthey saw,
An' cried that's fearfu' Wull o' the Raw.

Ne'er heed nae mair, the brasses I'll chip,
Wi' Pearson girnin' at my hip ;
A braw lord yet, I'll be that's shoor,
And think nae mair of Shafto Moor.
My lass sall be a lady grand,
Wi' diamond rings on every hand,
Her beautiful figure will grace my ha'
Then ye'll touch yer caps to Wull o' the Raw.

Haudaway Geordy.

Cum sit thou doon my canny lad,
   Th' trowth ta thou aw'll tell man ;
Aw'll let thou hear a canny bit sang
   A've meade aboot mawsel man.
Th' penny readins 'll seun be here,
   When aw'll sing leyke onie bordie ;
En when aw gie them th' graybord-hop,
   They'll a' shoot Haudaway Geordy.

KOROS.

Aw can kurb, en nick, en set a prop,
    En sing leyke onie bordie;
En when aw gie them th' graybord hop,
    They a' shoot Haudaway Geordy.

When aw gans in for a pint eh beer,
    Wad onie body think, man;
Sum shoots Geordy sing es a sang,
    En sum shoots Geordy, drink man.
Then aw sing th' Tinmith Trip,
    Or else the Hurdy Gurdy;
When they loup up aheet, en clap thor han's,
    En a' shoot Haudaway Geordy.

Wey, they talk iv Robin Burns's sangs,
    En Moore's, en wor Jim's tee, man;
En Ramsay's, Hogg's, en Tannahill's,
    Wey thor nut worth eh flee, man.
Me en maw marra when in at wark,
    At thaim we've tried wor hand, man,
Still thor's summick in thim yet
    We nivor can understand, man.

Thair's th' Lassie wi' th' Linty Locks,
    En th' bonnie hoos' iv Airlie;
On yon Hills are maw Fleecy Flocks,
    En ower the Wetter to Chairlie.

En Skott it did for Wallace bleed,
  En the Braes abean Benawe, man;
Th' Keelder Hunt en Wanny's en a',
  Hu, thor nout leyke sangs et a' man.

Bit thors yen thay ca' th' Big Meat Pie,
  Man it mun be a stunner;
En if aw nobbit hed that sang,
  Aw'l gar them laff leyke thunner.
En when thay shoot back, cum back,
  Aw gie them, nu let me see, man,
That's it begocks, aw hev hor noo,
  Aw'll gie them aw's on th' spree, man.

It wis doon at th' Faastean last year,
  When on th' stage thay gat ma;
Aw hard them say that's eh canny leyke lad,
  En th' lasses a' leukt at ma.
Then aw ga them the graybord hop,
  When the band play'd on th' Kordy;
Th' gam wis on when thay clapt thor han's,
  En a' shootit Haudaway Geordy.

On th' Tewsday last at fower o'clock,
  Aw gat eh grand luv letter,
Frev a canny lass, hor neam aw'll not tell,
  But aw knaw she leeves doon th' wetter,

Aye here it is thou can see for tha sel,
   It's hor han' maw cumley bordie;
In en oot, en roond aboot,
   It's a' ritten Haudaway Geordy.

If th' readins wis nobbit here agean,
   Thou'll see ma neam in th' papers;
Th' play-hoos en threeator tee,
   They say av stopt their capers.
They'll tell when aw sang Jack's cum Back,
   En then the Hurdy Gurdy;
Hoo aw finisht up wi' th' graybord hop,
   En they a' shootit Haudaway Geordy.

Johnnie the Caller.

INSCRIBED TO JOHN DOVELIN, WITH HIS PERMISSION.

SOME sing of Johnnie the Ploughboy,
   And some of Johnnie the Bellman;
But rambling Johnnie frae Cumberland,
   He does them far excel, man.
Johnnie is just five feet three,
   Neither short nor taller;
Thirteen stane an' pund or twee,
   Johnnie the Plashetts Caller.

CHORUS.

Johnnie's a brick, wi' his thunnerin' stick
    He lays on like a waller;
Get up my cock, it's three o'clock,
    Cries Johnnie the Plashetts Caller.

Johnnie rises like a lark,
    Sae early in the morning;
To rouse the foreshift men to wark,
    The wildest weather scorning.
His club he swings sae bold and free,
    My boys, he is a mauler;
Locks and bolts, he makes them flee,
    Johnnie the Plashetts Caller.

Johnnie's been a roving blade,
    Been a' thro' France an' Spain, lad;
On board a British Man o' War,
    He's plough'd the raging main lad,
An thrasht our foes, you may suppose,
    Tho' Johnnie is nae brawler;
On land an' wave a hero brave,
    Is Johnnie the Plashetts Caller.

Johnnie's ship she went wreck,
    To the boats they had to fly, lad;
The gallant crew sae brave and true
    Cast lots who had to die, lad.

The fatal lot on Johnnie fell,
    O, then blame him who can, lad,
He jumpt into the raging sea,
    And swam to the Isle o' Man, lad.

Johnnie can make a raspin' speech,
    An' tells o' sharks and whales, lad;
Great gorillas, crocodiles,
    An' big sea-serpents' tails, lad.
Bears an' lions, tigers too,
    Faix, Johnnie is nae drawler,
But boldly stands and waves his hands,
    Hurrah for Johnnie the Caller.

The Streams o' the West.

The publication of the following song in the *Hexham Herald*, May 18th, 1872, originated a poetical controversy, chiefly between Mr. James Anderson, the bard of Throckley, and the Author, in which several poets of no mean order took an active part.

The poems composing the controversy appeared partly in *The North of England Advertiser, Newcastle Weekly Chronicle*, and *Hexham Herald*. The Author considers himself justified, in vindication of his rights, in inserting the poems; and he sincerely trusts that, should his readers feel any repugnance at the strong invec- used in his replies, they will bear in mind that his opponent attacked him in a most unmanly and covert manner, hinting at the Author's family misfortune in such pointed language as to rouse and call forth the innermost ire of every true man's heart.

We'll away to the West, where the lavrock on high
Is singing a love song o' sweet liberty,

Where the wild thyme smells sweetly on yon bonnie glen,
An' the noops grow in plenty round the fell foxes' den.
We'll away up by Wannup, where the fleecy flocks feed,
We'll fish the White Kielder, the Jed, an' the Reed,
Where there's fine yellow trouts, lad, and fishing the best,
Away in the bonnie clear Streams o' the West.

Then seek out thy tackle, thy creel, an' thy gad,
An' we'll ower the mosses sae lightsome an' glad,
Where the wild heather-bleater on high quivering wing,
An' curlew an' plover gars a' the fells ring;
Where the blackcock croos proud on his ain benty knowe,
An' the wee grey mosscheeper trills cheerie, I trow;
O but it's gladsome on the mountain's wild crest,
Away by the bonnie clear Streams o' the West.

An' then there's the Esk an' the Liddel sae fine,
The Slitrig, the Teviot, an' bonnie North Tyne,

The Ewes, an' the Yarrow, an' Ettrick an' a',
Comes wimplin' by monie a fair flow'ry shaw;
Where we'll fling the flee lightly in linn and in stream,
An' twirl the trout deftly when his yellow fins gleam;
While the throssel sings clear to his mate in her nest,
Away by the bonnie clear Streams o' the West.

Sae blythesome we'll wander where the dew's sparkling sheen
Is shimmering in grandeur on the fairy-like scene,
Where the primrose peeps out frae the moss-covered brae,
An' the cowslip an' gowan sae lovely to see.
When the sun hides his glory, ance mair in our dreams
The bright spangl'd beauties we'll wile frae the streams,
Then joyfu' we'll wauken frae Nature's sweet breast,
Away by the bonnie clear Streams o' the West.

JAMES ARMSTRONG.

Plashetts.

The Banks o' the Tyne.

(Being a Reply to James Armstrong's " Streams o' the West.")

O Armstrong, dear brother, why boast o' yer dreams
About wild hills o' Wannup, an' clear western streams?
Ye boast o' yer hills an' yer green mossy fell,
Thinkin' nae ane can boast o' the like but yersel;
Ye boast o' the plover, the moorcock, and hen,
Where the wild thyme smells sweetly in yon bonnie glen;
Ye boast o' the lavrock as singin' sae fine,
While we claim the syem on the banks o' the Tyne.

O, the banks o' the Tyne are weel knawn far and near
For their beautiful landscapes and streams running clear;
Where the trout fills yer eyes with a gold-spangled gleam,
And the salmon glides swift through the bonnie clear stream;

Where the hills are all clad with the furze bush and trees;
Where down the deep glen blows the sweet western breeze;
Where the May flower, the wild rose, and bonny woodbine,
Send forth their sweet breath on the banks o' the Tyne.

Where the fruit blossom's verdure there's nought can surpass,
And the daisy would soften a heart made o' brass;
Where the cowslip and primrose peep out in the dell;
Where Nature's own self seems delighted to dwell;
Where the winter-sick world seems delighted to gaze,
And the critic's keen eye there will meet with amaze;
Where fortune and sunshine united do shine,
On the green grassy hills on the banks o' the Tyne.

But how does it happen, dear brother Armstrang,
That the fair-sex is scarce ever nyem'd in yer sang?
The real masterpiece o' Dame Nature's fine hand—

How could ye miss out, man, an idea sae grand?
The fairest o' flowers that shoot frae the stems—
The greatest of blessings,—the purest of gems;
With a fair virtuous woman sweet comforts will shine
Alike in the west and the banks o' the Tyne.

The roses may bloom, and the woodbine may climb,
The lambkins may sport in the height of their prime,
The daisy, the pink, and the primrose may spring,
The lavrock may soar to the clouds on the wing,
The Mayflower may bloom on the green crested thorn,
And the western breeze sport with the green waving corn,
But the country-bred lassie will all these outshine,
On the green mossy fells on the banks o' the Tyne.

JAMES ANDERSON.

Throckley, June 2, 1872.

North of England Advertiser, June 8, 1872.

Northumbria's Pride.

Inscribed to the Author of "The Wild Hills o' Wannys."

TUNE: "Humours o' Glen."

Oh, Armstrong, how sweetly ye strike the wild lyre,
    Ye gild ilka stream wi' a halo sae grand;
Your sweet hamely sangs set my bosom on fire,
    Wi' langing to feel the warm grasp o' your hand.
But tell me, dear Jamie, my muse-loving brither,
    Why leave oot the gem frae yer poetic dreams?
Ye may search lang and sair, but ye'll ne'er find anither
    Mair pure than the Coquet, the queen o' a' streams.

Auld Coquet can boast o' her wild rugged mountains,
    As grand as your "Wannie's" or Kielder's green knowes,
An' a thousand clear rills oozing creep fra' their fountains
    'Mang saft lintie blossoms that wave o'er the flowes.

Ilk bard o' auld Tyne may rejoice in its glory,
    An' brag o' its vales clad wi' posies sae fair,
An' sing o' its heroes an' auld castles hoary,
    But nane o' them a' can wi' Coquet compare.

They boast o' their "Staward" where nature rejoices,
    An' chant o' their glens an' ilk wee wimplin' burn;
But our streams, rills, an' birdies wi' sweet joyful voices,
    Trill'd sweetly a welcome when Coughron was born.
Yet lang, lovely Coquet, hast thou been neglected,
    I'm wae for to see thee left oot i' the cauld,
To gaze on ilk scene on thy bosom reflected,
    Will aye warm my heart tho' I'm weary an' auld.

How sweetly thou glides in thy sweet silvery beauty,
    Through groves where Pomona might sigh to repose;
Thou scoops out thy course where there's nought to pollute thee,
    As on to the ocean thou murmuring flows.

Entranced wi' the prospect, mute, muse-struck,
  I've listened
 To melodies sweet by ilk breeze borne alang,
While on ilka meadow pure crystal drops glistened,
An' hung frae ilk flow'ret in clusters sae thrang.

We've vales in the North, Jim, an' braes deck'd
  wi' flowers,
 Where dog-rose an' sweet fragrant woodbine
  entwine;
We breathe Heaven's pure air in our ain cozie
  bowers,
 Can ony say that on the banks o' the Tyne?
We have hills tow'rin' lofty, an' streams clear
  as onie,
 Whilk ripple alang o'er ilk pebble-clad bed;
We have woods waving green, and we've Loughs
  braid an' bonnie,
An' spots where the faes o' Northumbria have
  bled.

Then gie me your hand, Jim, there's joy yet
  before us,
 We've pleasures the dull, soulless worldlin'
  ne'er kens;
We taste bliss complete when the soft thrilling
  chorus
  O' nature's wild sang-birds ring through the
   deep glens.

Your sangs thrill my bosom, tho' coofs may deride them,
An' saut melting tears aften ooze frae my e'e.
They creep down my cheek, tho' I'm fain for to hide them,
  As in ilk ither line mair hame beauties I see.

Though critics may snarl, still their lash canna' harm ye,
  Just laugh while they choke wi' their spleen and abuse;
In return, Jim, the sweet smiles o' Clio will warm ye,
  An' scatter the darts o' the faes o' the muse.
May ye lang sing o' streams ye affirm are the clearest,
  An' soar o'er the crest o' adversity's tide,
But spare me ae toast for the stream I love dearest,
  'Tis Coquet, sweet Coquet, Northumbria's pride.

Lewis Proudlock.

Ridsdale.

Hexham Herald, June 15, 1872.

Bonnie North Tyne.

Ye hills where the clear winding streams o' the west
Rin wimplin' awa' o'er the wild mountain's crest,
An' birdies flit lightly the green leaves amang,
Or warble wi' Armstrang a saul-thrilling sang;
Though far frae the scenes that enrapture me still,
And while fancy neglects na, her flight ever will.
Oh! the wild heaving Wannies, like robins lang syne,
Are blent in my bosom wi' bonny North Tyne.

Untutor'd by art imperfections to hide,
There Nature exults in her grandeur and pride,
And flings her broad mantle o'er moorland and lea;
Where lambkins are sporting sae blithesome and free,
Oh! there let me ponder, and pensively stray
Through groves and green arbours the lang simmer day,
And muse, while at eve on my couch I recline,
O'er the wild heaving Wannies and bonny North Tyne.

Though fearfu' the frown o' the bleak northern
    sky,
And cheerless thine aspect as winter wins nigh,
How witching thy waters and woodlands appear
When ilka breeze whispers the spring-tide is
    near;
Then dewy the daisy peeps out frae the dell,
Where songsters a tale fu' o' tenderness tell.
Oh! Armstrang, dear brither, what then can
    outshine
The wild heaving Wannies and bonny North
    Tyne.

But time presses on, an' I canna weel spare
A moment frae duty to rhyme onie mair;
Syne theme of my heart for a season fareweel—
What aw canna express, like my betters, I feel;
And though I may never set fit on thy shore,
Nor wander thy wave-mirror'd banks as of yore,
Deep, deep shall the course of affection enshrine
The wild heaving Wannies and bonny North
    Tyne.

JOHN TURNBULL.

Shull Lodge.
Hexham Herald, June 22nd, 1872.

The Charms of the Coquet.

(An answer to James Armstrong's "Clear Streams o' the West," and James Anderson's "Banks o' the Tyne,")

O, ye crack o' yer hills and your streams o' the Wes',
And ye brag o' the grandeur in which they are drest,
And ye boast o' your lasses, sae bonnie and fine,
That grace the rich banks o' your famed coaly Tyne.
But frae hame wad ye gan, it's then ye wad ken
There are hills, dales, and streams that will match wi' your ain,
Where our rosy-cheeked lassies like fair flowers shine;
They may challenge the West, and the world renowned Tyne.

And then we have lavrocks that cheerily sing,
We've blackbirds and thrushes that can gar the woods ring;

Nay, our hills, dales, and streams, wi' Nature
    are drest:
Can the Tyne boast o' mair, or the streams o' the
    West?
By the streams o' the Coquet I love much to
    roam,
For there lies my fancy, and there stands my
    home,
To cheer me in need, when by sorrow oppressed,
And we baith love the Tyne, and the streams o'
    the West.

While the sun is up, and the morning is fine,
And the dewdrops on flowers like diamonds
    shine,
And each bird cheers his mate in the grove,
While the breeze skips alang wi' the sighs o'
    their love,
We'll away to yon hills where the curlews scream,
And we'll peep at the trout as they sport in the
    stream,
Where the shepherd tends flocks by the moun-
    tain's crest,
And Nature smiles by the streams o' the West.

We'll traverse the Kielder, and view grandeur
    fine,
We'll keek into the linty's nest on the banks o'
    the Tyne,

Yet we'll not rob her o' her young to grieve her breast,
And turn her to sighs by the streams o' the West.
But we'll soothe the heart, we'll smile with the gay,
Till the evening disrobes the bright orb of day.
Then like the sun, we'll retire to rest,
While Nature still blooms by the streams o' the West.

Rothbury, June 12, 1872.
North of England Advertiser, June 29, 1872.

The Queen of the Flowers.

On reading " The Streams of the West," and " The Banks of the Tyne."

Let Armstrong, our brother, indulge in his dreams
Of the wild hills of Wanny, and the clear western streams;
Let him boast of the mountains and fells clad with bent;
Let him boast of the heath to his heart's full content.

No wonder he boasts of the streams of the west,
For each thinks his own country-side far the best.
He can boast of his mossy and heather-clad moors,
But no praise has he found for the Queen of the Flowers.

He can boast of the plovers and sky-larks that sing
Their sweet songs in the morn as they soar on the wing.
If the landscape his bosom with happiness fills,
And he pleasure can find in Northumbria's hills;
If he boast not the flower that adorns most our cot,
The choicest of gems, then I envy him not:
For this rich, lovely gem we can proudly call ours—
'Tis the pride of the earth and the Queen of the Flowers.

We will boast of the good and the virtuous fair,
And assert there is nothing with them can compare
The glittering diamond is compared of no worth
With a pure-minded woman, the gem of the earth.

No wonder, friend Anderson, thou should demand
How he could miss out an idea so grand.
She cheers with her presence life's gloomiest hours,
And claims as her right to be Queen of the Flowers.

He may boast, if he will, of his long range of sight,
As he gazes afar from black Belling's proud height;
He may boast of his wilds; to the song birds may raise
As high as the mountains his voice in their praise;
But a virtuous woman, my friend, is a prize
That he well might extol to the blue vaulted skies.
He might fancy his hills were the fairest of bowers
If they were but adorn'd with the Queen of the Flowers.

THOMAS WALL.

Gosforth, June, 1872.
Newcastle Weekly Chronicle, June 29, 1872.

Anither Sang.

(In the Newcastle Dialect.)

In answer te that Throckley chep. Syem teun as
"Haudaway Geordy."

Whei hinny, Jamie, hawd thaw hand
An' howay get thy bate, man,
Thou'll spoil the score pryce varra seun
If thou hews it sic a rate man;
Hoots man, hawd on, let s hev a low,
Put on thaw sark an' coat, man,
An' we'll hev a crack iboot thor sangs;
They tell me thou's a pote man.

   Koris—Then set thawsel away for fair,
    An' praise thaw weel-knawn river,
    Thou has no call te hew ne mair,
    Ned Renwick sáys thou's clivor.

Thou says aw boast iboot ma hills,
An' bonny western streams, man,
Moorcocks an' hens an' bonny glens
It aw saw in maw dreams, man.

Eigh aw've fisht monie a sparklin' stream,
An' clumb the hills se hee, man,
An' aw wul sing iboot them yit
Until the day aw dee, man.

An' then thou tells ov thaw green hills
Alang the banks iv Tyne, man,
The Mayflo'er an' the weyld rose, te,
An' wudbine smellin' fine, man.
Bit ov the smells iv Lemmintin
Thou nivor yence did speak, man,
An' thou hes mist a nidee grand
Iboot the Wylam reek, man.

Thou tells iboot that grand fur tree
Besyde thaw nobil rivor;
When thou boasts ov thaw lassis, te,
Thou caps me clean hoosivor.
Noo thraw thaw picks and drills away,
Shot-box, an' canny pit claes, man,
An' smash thaw cracket a' te bits,
An' myek sangs a' thaw days, man.

Is seun is thou kan git away
Cum te the West, maw laddy,
An' we'll gan an' see that Coquet chep
An' the shephord an' his pladdy.

Man if thou saw the heathor bells
An' hard the whusslin plivor,
Thou wad think't fair hivin on the fells,
An' leave Sooth Tyne for ivor.

JAMES ARMSTRONG.

Plashetts.

North of England Advertiser, June 29, 1872.

Another Song

IN ANSWER TO JAMES ARMSTRONG.

AIR: "There's nae luck aboot the hoose."

Noo, Armstrong, aw hev seen yor sang,
   An' prood aw was te read it ;
An' may yor life continue lang
   Te write the sangs that's needed.
About hewin thoo hes shaved me clean,
   Ne doot thou thinks't a mazer ;
But before thoo tries to shave agyen,
   Aw hope thou'll whet thy razor.

Chorus.

So try an' blaw anuther breeze,
   An' divvent miss the mark, man ;
But write of lasses, flowers, an' trees,
   An' miss oot dirty wark, man.

Aw nivor·interfere wi' wark,
    At least when aw is writin;
For aw nivor think it's worth the time,
    Nor trouble ov inditin.
Gud subjects we can find bi scores,
    Throughout the whole creashun ;
So try agyen and choose a yen
    That better suits thy stashun.

Thoo says, aw nivor nyem the smoke
    Ov Lemminton an' Wylam;
Wey! thou surely thinks aw've just cum oot
    A lunatic asylum.
When aw write sangs aw try to praise
    Things worthy ov attenshun;
But te write ov smoke an' boast ov wark
    Such things aw'll nivor menshun.

Thoo says thoo's fish'd i' mony a stream,
    Wey! we differ there agyen man,
Te kill a fish, or owt else, thoo
    Must hev a heart o' styen man ;
Aw cuddent treed a daisy doon,
    Nor anything alarm, man ;
Aw cuddent treed upon a worm,
    A moose aw cuddent harm, man.

Noo aw'll conclude an' thenk ye
  For yor kindly invitashun,
Te see the west i' nature drest
  Is indeed maw inclinashun.
So adieu! till aw can see a chance,
  For us twe lads te meet, man,
An' ower a glass, wor sangs discuss,
  An' spend a jolly neet, man.
                              JAMES ANDERSON.
Throckley.
Hexham Herald, 6th July, 1872.

Anither Sang.

IN REPLY TO ANDERSON'S "CANNY TYNESIDE."

Anderson, my mannie, I've seen a graun sang,
That ye threep is your ain, be it richt or wrang,
Whilk ye've made a' yersel' when ye coull hae been seen
A-wanderin' the road aboot Wa'bittle Dene.

Chorus.

It 'ill kythe on ye, Jimmie, an' that 'ill be seen,
Gin ye tak thae wanderin's by Wa'bittle Dene.

O Jimsie, O Jimsie, say hoo did ye feel,—
Was ye lauchin', or greetin', or was ye no weel?

Was ye luve-sick, or meun-struck? O tell me
    skrahean;
Or what gars ye wander by Wa'bittle Dene?

Then tell me, my laddie, when ye tuk the fit—
Was ye on the fuddle or down in the pit?
Or courtin' the lasses, o' whilk yer sae keen,
Or wanderin' the road aboot Wa'bittle Dene.

If luve ails ye, Jimmie, then tak' Lang Will's
    plan,
An' work'd aff wi' physic as seun as ye can;
Yer a queer ane, deed are ye, to be sae aft seen
A-wanderin the road aboot Wa'bittle Dene.

Or gin ye be meun-struck, then hasten wi' speed,
An' get a cauld kail-blade, an' lay on yer head,
A neep-shaw, or docken, or aucht that is green,
When ye tak thae wanderin's by Wa'bittle Dene.

Tak' my advice, noo, an' mind what I say,—
Get boor'd for the sturdy, and do not delay;
Or else some cauld mornin' they'll fin' ye, I ween,
Lyin' awelt and frozen by Wa'bittle Dene.

                        JAMES ARMSTRONG.

Plashetts.

"Hexham Herald," November 23rd, 1872

"Anither Sang."

In reply to Jimmie Armstrang's sturdy sang.

Oh, Armstrang, dear brother! whate'er can ye
    mean
By askin' such questions aboot Walbottle Dene?
For aw wander these roads when the Muses do
    move,
Without e'er bein' sea-sick wi' meunshine or love;
And while aw love lasses, and lasses love me,
Aw'll sing of their praises in each bank and brae;
And aw think it an honour to be often seen
In that famous old love depot, Walbottle Dene.

And as for the fuddlin' that's nyem'd in yer sang,
If that's yer idea yer a thousand miles wrang;
For though aw'll admit that aw like a quiet gill,
Aw ne'er liked yer fuddlin', and hope aw never
    will.
Ony good social company aw'll join in their thrang,
And de me best to assist wiv a toast or a sang,
But for lyin' oot at neets, man, aw've ne'er yet
    been seen,
Not e'en in my favourite spot, Walbottle Dene.

Or do ye think aw gan oot wi' the gun for me
    plan,
To slaughter dumb animals, or frighten frail man,
As Jim Westgarth tells me, when ye were wi'
    him,
The Pont keepers cam and compell'd ye to swim.
O no, maw dear man, when aw wander the lane,
It's not to cause any dumb animal pain,
But a-courtin' the Muse and admiring the scene
Of that dear auld romantic spot, Walbottle Dene.

So now, my brave fellow, aw'll finish me rhyme,
And aw hope that ye'll myek better use o' yer
    time:
And sing aboot lasses, and hills, woods, and dells,
Fine rivers and streamlets, and sweet heather
    bells.
And when ye gan forward Dame Nature to scan,
Just think o' the blessin' that woman's to man;
And then at a glance it is plain to be seen
The reason aw wander by Walbottle Dene.

                    JAMES ANDERSON.

Throckley, December 2, 1872.
"Hexham Herald," December 7, 1872.

The Duel.

Brave Anderson went to the toon,
    Wi' his cronies a' in clusters;
Bout pistils, guns, and twa lang swords,
    Baith double cut and thrusters,
What ails ye noo, Frank Maffen said,
    Are ye gaun ta shoot some fewil,
O! no lad, no, I'm a hero,
    I'm gaun ta feycht a Duel.

Chorus.

It's nae use tryin' to haud me noo,
    I'll kill that ootbye huel;
Just beyde off me, I'll let ye see,
    I'm gaun to feycht a Duel.

I'm gannin West to North Teyne heed,
    Wul ye gan wi" me my mannie;
I'll shoot that chiel o' Plashetts deed,
    Him the weyld herds ca' Wanny.
O! haud yer han', then Westgarth cried,
    An' dinna be sae cruel;
Ye'll dae nae guid to spill his blud,
    O! dinna feycht a Duel.

It's nae use taukin noo, its no,
  'He sal ken wi' wha he's dealin;
Bring me some poother an' some shot,
  An' yon lang gun frae Ponteelin.
Brave *Telford*, he'll stand at my back,
  Till I *slew* the heelin huel;
An' I'll never flinch a half an inch
  When I gan to feycht the Duel.

He put on that coat o' *Henderson's*,
  Fill'd a pocket fu' o' poother;
Put bullits, guns, caps, swords an' a',
  An' pistils in the t'other.
Then he went on to Throckley Fell,
  Wi' baggy Frank and Rowell,
And they put him thro' his exercise,
  To gan and feycht the Duel.

They put a yetlin on his heed,
  A horse tail on the middle;
At break o' day he maircht away,
  To the soond o' feyfe and fiddle.
Come back, come back, the auld weyves cried,
  O! come back, Jim, my jewel;
My lad, it'll wer doughters kill,
  If ye fa' in the Duel.

He maircht on still through Harlowhill,
  The colours ower him flyin;
The gewgaws an' tin-whussils played,
  There he left the lassies cryin.
The last teyme ever he was seen
  Was on the banks o' Ruel,
Shootin—hip hurray, noo clear the way,
  I'm gaun to feycht a Duel.

END OF THE CONTROVERSY.

CROSSING THE CHEVIOTS.

On the 8th of August, 1879, I went off to see my brother at Ford. Away up the Reed, by Otterburn, Bennett's Field, Steward Shields, Coquetside, up by Shillmoor, and from thence up the glen of the Usway to Usway Ford, where I stayed all night. In the morning it was a dark mist, and the herd got the horse and set me to Cocklaw Foot. My line was across the Cheviot, but as Henshole was enveloped in a misty cloud, my pilot strongly advised me not to venture over the heights, and as he had it, "It's a ruggit track ony way, and in the mist it's a thousand chances to ane again ye, as yer maist seer to get lost; but I can set ye on a safe track doon the Bowmont and roon by Yetholm." And as I was in a "swither" I took his advice. On arriving at Yetholm I inquired of a fair-haired lassie if ever she had seen the Gipsy Queen, and if she was a good crack. "Ow aye, monie a time. She's nae greet seycht ta see, but she'll tell ye a lot o' nonsense ta begin wi', an spae yer fortune by yer han'." Just then a butcher came up with his cart and gave me the chance of a ride (13 miles) canny man, so off we went, and on the way passed the Yeavering Bell, and the Field of Flodden, fatal Flodden. At last I arrived at Ford and had a few days' fishing, but nothing to crack on. Left my kind friends and Ford intending to come by Rothbury, but on coming to Millfield the fit came on me to cross the Cheviots, so off I started; crossed the Glen Water, up the College Burn, and over the "ruggit" track by Henshole, and as it was fine and clear I enjoyed a scene of wild and sublime grandeur that neither poet's pen nor painter's pencil can describe. Surely if there is a foretaste of Heaven it is on Cheviot on a clear summer's day. After gazing my fill on this mountain paradise I struck over to Usway ford. Welcome, a hearty welcome, from every one—kind souls the Andersons, both old and young. On Saturday, I was up in good time and pulled a fine lot of noops or cloud berries, then down to the house, and after many kindly invitations to come back and have a few days hunting, I took the road, and over by Barra Burn; stripped, and had a good labber in the Coquet, when I was as fresh as a lavrock, and footed it over the fells to bonnie Reedwater again.

www.ingramcontent.com/pod-product-compliance
Lightning Source LLC
Chambersburg PA
CBHW032157160426
43197CB00008B/962